Restraining the Wicked

The Dangerous Offender Project

JUSTICE

John P. Conrad and Simon Dinitz
Project Co-Directors
The Academy for Contemporary Problems

In Fear of Each Other John P. Conrad and Simon Dinitz
The Law and the Dangerous Criminal Linda Sleffel
The Search for Criminal Man Ysabel Rennie
The Violent Few Donna Martin Hamparian, Richard Schuster, Simon Dinitz, and John P. Conrad
Restraining the Wicked Stephan W. Van Dine, John P. Conrad, and Simon Dinitz
The Career of the Dangerous Criminal John P. Conrad, Simon Dinitz, and Stuart A. Miller
Out of Circulation: The Dangerous Offender in Prison Simon Dinitz, John P. Conrad, Israel Barak, and Robert Freeman
Felons in Court Winifred Lyday, John P. Conrad, and Simon Dinitz
The Dangerous and the Endangered John P. Conrad

Cover: Cuneiform characters for the word *Justice*, the emblem of the Dangerous Offender Project.

Restraining the Wicked

The Incapacitation of the Dangerous Criminal

Stephan Van Dine
Ohio Adult Parole Authority and
The Academy for
Contemporary Problems

John P. Conrad
American Justice Institute

Simon Dinitz
Ohio State University and
The Academy for
Contemporary Problems

Lexington Books
D.C. Heath and Company
Lexington, Massachusetts
Toronto

Library of Congress Cataloging in Publication Data

Van Dine, Stephan.
    Restraining the wicked.

    "The Dangerous offender project."
    Bibliography: p.
    Includes index.
    1. Imprisonment—United States. 2. Prison sentences—United States.
3. Crime prevention—United States. I. Conrad, John Phillips, 1913-   joint
author. II. Dinitz, Simon, joint author. III. Title.
HV8705.V36   365   77-10166
ISBN 0-669-01774-4

Published simultaneously in Canada

Printed in the United States of America

International Standard Book Number: 0-669-01774-4

Library of Congress Catalog Card Number: 77-10166

Contents

List of Figures and Tables

Preface

"Wicked people exist. Nothing avails except to set them apart from innocent people."

—James Q. Wilson

This conclusion by one of America's most influential social critics[1] prescribes a fundamental shift in the goals of criminal justice. Whatever these goals may have been in Anglo-American jurisprudence, the incapacitation of the wicked has never predominated, although certainly it has been one of the considerations that legislators have borne in mind in drafting laws, and judges have weighed in sentencing offenders. But to accord primacy to the objective of setting apart the wicked implies a major change in the ways in which we deal with offenders. Strict adherence to Professor Wilson's prescription will call for a new policy, the specifications of which have not been detailed nor the consequences estimated.

For the staff of the Dangerous Offender Project, Wilson's maxim presented an obvious challenge. Wickedness is not a precise term, but undoubtedly offenders who are dangerous qualify as members of such a class. Our concern with the dangerous criminal is purely academic if we cannot formulate recommendations for his improved control. A strategy for assessing the probable consequences for carrying out the policy recommended by Wilson—and many others—presented itself. The research on which we report in this book constitutes our assessment of these consequences.

It is an empirical study, so far as we know, the first that has been undertaken. Except in the last chapter, where we permit ourselves an extrapolation of our findings, we have adhered faithfully to the official data generated by the criminal justice agencies in Franklin County, Ohio, in which Columbus, the city in which we live and work, is situated.

It has been a difficult book to write. Throughout our study we have been acutely conscious of the controversy on the subject of incapacitation that has swirled through the criminal justice community. On the one hand, conservative advocates of policy change insist that the wicked should be removed from the community; on the other hand, liberal jurists and philosophers hold that those removed will be replaced by others until remedies are found for the inequities and grievances suffered by the losers in a poorly functioning social system.

Some of the preliminary findings of our research have been published elsewhere.[2] In these studies we laid out the results of tests of various sentencing options intended to reduce crime by incapacitating the violent offender. These reports have been interpreted in various ways according to the ideological perspective of our critics. Some argue that incapacitation is no more than a vogue in the discourse generated by the alarming increase in violent crime. Others point out that the exceedingly modest reduction in crime that we could firmly predict did not take account of the uncleared crimes that must have been committed by those who would be incapacitated by our various hypothetical sentences. The recent study by Silberman, *Criminal Violence, Criminal Justice*, adopts the former position, but we have had many critics who hew to the latter. The facts that we have assembled in this final report of our work still lean toward the former position, but we concede that if this country is willing to accept the immense social and economic costs of an incomparably severe sentencing policy, some noticeable reduction in crime can be achieved.

Our data were assembled to settle four different questions:

1. The effectiveness of different sentencing policies of varying severity in preventing violent crimes by incapacitating those who commit them at an earlier time.
2. The increase in prevention that would be achieved by including the juvenile records of violent adult offenders in the sentencing consideration.
3. The effectiveness of applying sentencing policies imposed on adult offenders to juvenile violent offenders.
4. The "false positive" effect: How many persons would be incapacitated unnecessarily by the administration of such a policy because they would not actually commit the violent offense for which they would be incarcerated?

We have our own answers to these questions, and we stand by them. We have not hesitated to state our views about the implications of these answers for the making of policy. The controversy will continue, but our contribution of data will at least provide an empirical cast to a debate that hitherto has been heavily speculative.

Notes

1. James Q. Wilson, *Thinking About Crime* (New York: Basic Books, 1975), p. 209.

2. See Stephan Van Dine, Simon Dinitz, and John P. Conrad, "The Incapacitation of the Dangerous Offender: A Statistical Experiment." *Journal of Research in Crime and Delinquency*, vol. 14, no. 1 (1977), 22-34.

Acknowledgments

A study of this kind is especially dependent on the help provided by agencies in possession of the files and records that constitute its data. For their patience and positive assistance, the law enforcement agencies of Franklin County deserve all the praise and gratitude that we can give them. These agencies include the Franklin County Prosecutor's Office, the Clerk of the Court of Common Pleas, the Sheriff's Department, the Columbus Police Department, the Adult Parole Authority of the Ohio Department of Rehabilitation and Correction, and the Ohio Youth Commission. They allowed us to use their files, explained what we could not immediately understand, and afforded indispensable answers to the puzzles we could not solve for ourselves. The study of aggravated assault provides an interesting example. More than 89 percent of these crimes were technically cleared, but we could find only 13 percent of those reported as winding up with an actual arrest. A discrepancy of this order will bring a statistician up short. The explanation, simple and demonstrable, was that in the case of family assaults the offender is identified, the case is closed, but the victim declines to prosecute. That so many grievously harmed individuals should forego the remedy of prosecution surprised us all, and testifies to considerations that somebody should explore further. For our purposes, the integrity of our data could not be assured without explanation. Not an isolated example; what we had to know was explained by our colleagues in the police and the courts.

The cooperation of George Smith, the Franklin County prosecutor, and of his executive assistant, William Curlis, was indispensable. We had to rely on records explained to us by James Lucks of the Criminal Division of the Office of the Clerk of the Franklin County Court of Common Pleas. Sheriff Harry Berkemer and his assistant, Sergeant Robert Mohr, facilitated the collection of arrest data. At the Adult Parole Authority, Nick Gatz, then superintendent of administration and research, now supervisor of community services, and Ray Capots, his successor, were helpful in amplifying our data.

The cooperation extended by Chief Earl Burden of the Columbus Police Department was crucial. With his authorization, Sergeant Donald Raabe collected the adult criminal histories for us, and Sergeant John Phillips and Mrs. Helen Spires searched the juvenile arrest files.

We had to have access to files maintained by the Ohio Youth Commission and must acknowledge the generous assistance of Director William Willis, his deputy, Gerald Novack, and staff members Dr. Alice Carter and Jim Pugliesi.

The active interest and encouragement of President Ralph Widner of The Academy for Contemporary Problems was an essential ingredient of whatever success this study may enjoy. Willing assistance was provided by our conscientious and capable staff, particularly the painstaking collation of data by Evalis Lemberg-Jacobsen, Nikki Borman, and Brenda Chaney. Donna Hamparian, a colleague in all our studies, was a reliable source of information, especially about the juvenile justice system, and provided helpful criticisms when we could use them. So did Ysabel Rennie, who participated in the conceptualization of our investigation. Sherry Flannery, our incomparable secretary, made the difficult easy, and saw to it that deadlines were met in spite of last minute changes of direction and content. Lois Gaber, acting as an auxiliary, cheerfully did more than was expected or required.

This research began in a graduate seminar in systems analysis in the School of Public Administration at the Ohio State University. It evolved into a policy paper supervised by Professor Robert Backoff. Many others in the School contributed to the development of the plan for the study, and we particularly express our gratitude to Dr. Eric Carlson, Frank Marshall, and Susan Lowe for their contributions.

The data analysis was competently handled by Donald Smeltzer of the Department of Psychiatry and his associates Steven Luce and Raechel Napier. The analysis on which the false-positive component was based was carried out by Richard Haller and his associates at the Mershon Center. The peculiar requirements of this study called for no little ingenuity, and Smeltzer and Haller provided what was required.

Valuable critiques of our work were offered and published by Jan Palmer and John Salimbene, and by Barbara Boland. Their disagreement with our conclusions served to broaden the scope of our research. David Greenberg gave us useful comments and advice, as did Joan Petersilia. She and Peter Greenwood of the Rand Institute later replicated our study with data from Denver, Colorado, and we were gratified that their results were closely comparable to our first published study.

Above all, the material support of the Lilly Endowment of Indianapolis and the encouragement provided by Richard Ristine and Charles Blair were fundamental to the completion of the project. We doubt that many researchers have enjoyed such patient and understanding sponsorship.

Supplementary funding was afforded at a critical time by the Administration of Justice Division of the Ohio Department of Economic and Community Development. We must thank Dr. Bennett Cooper and Charles Scales of that agency for making this assistance possible. We must also acknowledge the many ways in which Margaret Zusky of Lexington Books and her staff have facilitated the metamorphosis of an idea into this book.

Our wives have been well conditioned to the irregular hours and the abstracted moods that work of this kind entails. Somehow they weathered the storms this study occasioned, and maintained their good humor throughout. We are sure that they are as pleased as we are that it is out of the way and into print. The thanks we offer to Ellen Schneider, Mim Dinitz, and Charlotte Conrad are a lot more than a mere formality.

It is said that many hands make light work, and we wish we could say that it's true. There were many hands involved in this book, and credit goes to all of them for whatever we have done well. Our oversights and gaffes have been committed within our special circle of three, and none of us is in a position to project the blame beyond that circle.

1 Introduction

Speculations on the Prevention of Crime

More than other social institutions, criminal justice is afflicted with tangled imperatives. On the threshold of their careers, beginning penologists learn that the tangle is created by a conflict between society's impulse to retaliate against the offender by hurting him for the wrong he has done and its wish to help him so that he will not do it again. Throughout most of human history, the impulse to hurt has been far in the ascendant; it is only during the last 200 years that serious thought has been given to measures which might help the offender. During the decades since World War Two many factors have contributed to the hope that wise penal intervention might restore criminals to society by helping them rather than to consign them to precarious lives on the margin. Those hopes are fading. Studies of rehabilitative programs have given no reason for confidence that they can bring about the changes necessary to convert criminals into citizens.[1]

Disillusion with the rehabilitative ideal has turned attention back to the inhibiting effects of punishment. Mathematicians and economists have been spurred to assess the effectiveness of general deterrence, that is, to assess the extent to which the infliction of punishment on actual offenders may discourage potential offenders from trying their luck. Such research must always contain too many elements of speculation to be wholly convincing, but it is noteworthy that the effectiveness of deterrence is no longer to be taken for granted, as was the case in all former years, but now is to be assessed through the application of mathematical models.[2]

The inhibiting effect of incapacitation has attracted at least as much attention. Speculation by law enforcement officials and commentators has stressed the plausible notion that a criminal in full-time custody will commit no crimes in the community.[3] Mathematicians have created models for estimating the degree to which crime rates might be diminished by sentencing felons more stringently. The models have convinced some theorists that these reductions would be enough to justify major changes in sentencing policy. James Q. Wilson estimated that more severe incapacitation of "convicted serious robbers" would make possible a 20 percent reduction in the rate of robbery, and conceivably even larger reductions.[4] Ernest Van den Haag went further to propose "post-punishment confinement" for the further protection of society.[5] Both writers and their mathematical colleagues assumed that most apprehended criminals have perpetrated numerous crimes for which they have not been apprehended. This opinion is supported by common sense, the informed belief of police officers, and by the responses to questionnaires administered to convicts concerning their unreported criminal histories.[6] These studies of self-reported criminal histories invariably turn up a large amount of previously uncleared crime. In the mind of the speculative social critic it therefore follows that crime rates can be drastically reduced simply by locking up more criminals for longer periods of time.

Speculation has often been the curse of criminal justice policy formulation. Some mathematical model builders have found it more convenient to consider the responses of the rational man to the administration of the laws than to deal with the complexities of a system appropriate to the patterns of criminal man and at the same time compatible with the ideal of equal justice. The criminal man is not to be mistaken for the rational man of the economist or the reasonable, prudent man of jurisprudence. The ebb and flow of criminality in an advanced society will not obey the rules that govern other social phenomena. The benefits of a criminal act and the costs of its consequences do not conform to rational processes of calculation in the mind of a dope-addicted hoodlum as they will in the balance sheets of a business entrepreneur. Too often the handy analogies drawn from the economic theory, or even from fields of social deviance other than criminal behavior, turn out to be useless in understanding and controlling crime.

But speculative policy-making has had a long and impressive impact on criminal justice. Data for reference in assessing the past or planning the future have only recently become available in volume. The original theory on which modern penology is based in Europe and North America must be credited to Jeremy Bentham, who, whether he intended it or not, has by far the best claim to be the father of penal doctrine. Though he freely gave credit to the reformative efforts of John Howard, who staunchly expounded civilized standards in the administration of jails, it was Bentham who formulated the purposes and proposed the structure of the penal apparatus as we know it today. As a theorist, he was the creature of his times. The French Enlightenment ordered his perspective and instilled a predilection for rationality in the management of human affairs. Revolted by the hideous methods that prevailed throughout Europe and that had been so well documented by Howard, Bentham was impelled to put his extraordinarily active mind to the task of designing a system that would replace the numerous hangings of a considerable variety of felons, and the consignment of thousands of others to noisome old ships moored in the Thames. The system would, of course, be derived from and integrated with the Utilitarian ethic which was Bentham's life-work, whereby public policy was to be formulated in accordance with calculations of what was needed to achieve the greatest happiness of the greatest number; this is the Greatest Happiness Principle, the keystone of Utilitarianism. A summary of Bentham's countless ideas about crime and punishment would be an impractical digression, but what he had to say about the incapacitation of dangerous offenders is relevant as a statement of his original thought about the effectiveness of incarceration in reducing the volume of crime:

> With respect to any particular delinquent, we have seen that punishment has three objects: incapacitation, reformation, and intimidation. If the crime he has committed is of a kind calculated to inspire great alarm, as manifesting a very mischievous disposition, it becomes necessary to take from him the power of committing it again. But if the crime, being less dangerous, only justified transient punishment, and it is possible for a delinquent to return to society, it is proper that the punishment should possess qualities calculated to reform or intimidate him.[7]

It was obvious to Bentham that a long term of imprisonment would prevent the criminal so detained from committing crimes. He had no compunctions about life term sentences for malefactors whose incarceration would be perpetual—in prisons painted black to "inspire salutary terrors" in youths who might visit such places.[8] Bentham's notions about human beings and their behavior had a mechanical quality, rather like those of some modern behaviorists who suppose that everyone responds identically to identical stimuli. But he was an innovator who saw that more than good intentions would be necessary to reform the prevailing system of punishing criminals. Rationality had to be introduced, and Bentham knew that he was the first thinker with sufficient stamina to give the problems of crime and punishment the detailed attention they required.

It is too much to attribute the entire course of penology to Bentham's influence, but most of the ideas which have dominated thought about crime and punishment can be found in his prolix codification (Bentham's own coined word) of the principles of penal law. He understood very well that he was the pioneer in thought about these matters; he dismissed his predecessors, who included such illustrious names as Montesquieu, d'Alembert, and Beccaria, as without method or direction by general principle. He is little read now, but his influence on liberalizing legislation of many kinds was enormous throughout the nineteenth century in the western world. We are still Benthamites; the Panopticon that he conceived to be the solution to the crime problem was considered an impractical extravagance in England, (though it was faithfully built in Stateville, Illinois), but the prison as an alternative to savage barbarism in the administration of justice survives with its three functions of incapacitation, reformation, and intimidation, just as he prescribed. The same distinction stands between the chronic, dangerous offenders who must be incapacitated, and the less dangerous offenders who need only to be reformed or intimidated. However obvious these concepts may seem to us, we have to keep in mind their novelty to Bentham's contemporaries, many of whom were certain that the death penalty had to be retained for all felonies if British subjects were to be safe in their homes and on their streets.

Incapacitation has had its place in theorizing about punishment, of which there has been a great deal, ever since Bentham's time. Until recently, incarceration to restrain the offender has been regarded as subsidiary to the great aims of retributive justice. We dissent vigorously from the version of retributivism laid down by that thunderous nineteenth century judge Sir James Fitzjames Stephen, but we concede his point in the following excerpt from his *History of the Criminal Law in England:*

> [In addition to retribution] another object [of legal punishment] is the direct prevention of crime, either by fear, or by disabling or even destroying the offender, and this which is, I think, commonly put forward as the only proper object of legal punishment is beyond all question distinct from the one just mentioned and of coordinate importance with it. The two objects are in no degree inconsistent with each other, on the contrary they go hand in hand, and may be regarded respectively as the secondary and the primary effects of the administration of justice. The only practical result in the actual administration of justice of admitting each as a separate ground for punishment is that when a discretion as to the punishment of an offense is placed in a judge's hands, as it is in almost all cases by our law, the judge in the exercise of that discretion ought to have regard to the moral guilt of the offence as well as to its specific public danger.[9]

Sir James was not a man who was inclined to doubt; he knew a public danger when he saw it, and he had no reservations about his duty as a judge to protect the public from it. Although we share his concern for the protection of the public, we live in an age of crumbled certainties. We do not know exactly who is dangerous, or how long any dangerous individual must be considered to be dangerous. Unlike Sir James, we hope to find out by empirical methods. The mathematical models that have inspired some of our contemporaries require a diet of facts if they are to be useful to those who would prescribe or make policy. Without them, no model builder is in a better position than Bentham or Stephen or hundreds of forgotten judges and legislators whose certitudes came from the common sense of comfortable life in the seats of power.

Policy-makers must test their assumptions on the data of the crime they hope to reduce. The excoriations of criminal statistics in this country are staple clichés of social research. It is remarkable to read denunciations of their inadequacies preceding their use as forage for the computer, for want of truly valid data. As to the regularly compiled statistical reports of crime, the scorn of the critics is founded in defective methods and control by the compilers. What is needed, and where the official reports will not do, is the specific collection of data for specific answers to specific questions. The traditions of criminology are rich in just this kind of research. The publication of the *Uniform Crime Reports* series led to efforts to arrive at macrosocial conclusions about crime rates, principally by economists who supposed that these rates would be subject to the same analytic methods that they applied to rates of economic growth.

We have chosen to collect our own data for this study of the effect of incapacitation on crime rates. Our primary sources were the files of the Columbus, Ohio Police Department and the Franklin County Court of Common Pleas. Our questions were simple, and the official records proved to be fully adequate for our limited purposes. We reasoned that if effective restraint of criminals would reduce the rate of crime, then those offenders who appear in court today would not have committed their crimes had they been in captivity at the time their offenses were committed.

It followed that if we could obtain the criminal histories of the offenders who were arrested during some specific year—we chose 1973—and imposed an imaginary prison sentence on them at the time of their last felony conviction (if any), we could make some estimates about the amount of crime that would thereby be prevented, *and about the amount of crime that could not be prevented by incapacitating sentences.*

Because our project was directed at an understanding of the dangerous offender, we limited the study to those violent offenders who were arrested during 1973. There were 364 of them. Eliminating fourteen whose crimes were committed in prison, and eight for whom no criminal histories—"rap sheets"—could be found, we were left with a study population of 342 persons charged as adults with one or more of the "index" crimes of violence: homicide, forcible rape, aggravated assault, and robbery. Within this population, 166 had been found guilty in court as charged. The remaining 176 were either released after pleas of *nolle prosequi* or pled guilty to lesser offenses after negotiations with the County Prosecutor. (See chapter 3, pages 46-47, for an explanation of *nolle prosequi.*)

Our first question was: Assuming that everyone in the whole population under study was guilty as charged—even if they were not—how many of them could not have committed the crime with which they were charged if a prison sentence had been imposed on them when they last were convicted in court? We then broke down this question to determine how many of those actually convicted of a violent offense might have been thwarted from the commission of that offense by a previously imposed sentence to prison.

As we shall recount in detail in later chapters, we were able to imagine a great variety of possible sentences, beginning with the manifestly impractical sentence of five years flat for any felony, regardless of its gravity and regardless of the offender's age. Thirty-five other sentencing alternatives were imposed with varying results, though none of them were as preventive as the implacable five years which we took to be beyond the limits of tolerable severity and the economical administration of criminal justice.

Any study of this kind will suffer by dividing adult from juvenile crime. We knew perfectly well that juvenile offenders commit a very large number of violent crimes. If incapacitation were to be treated as a strategy of crime control, we would have to take into account the juvenile records of our younger adult offenders—those who were under the jurisdiction of the juvenile court at some time during the five years preceding their 1973 offense. Because the Federal Bureau of Investigation does not assemble criminal histories before offenders reach adult years, our data collection had to be approached by way of the police records for juvenile arrests and the dispositions of the juvenile court. We imposed the same battery of fictitious sanctions on the juveniles who eventually matured into our study population, even though American criminal justice has always moderated the punishment meted out to children.

Some violent crime is committed by early adolescents, though, as we showed in the earlier book of this series, *The Violent Few*, the incidence is not as high as generally supposed, nor is the severity of the offenses committed as great. To test the usefulness of incapacitation as a policy for the reduction of juvenile violence, we applied the same concept of the fictitious but severe sentence that we used to test the effectiveness of incapacitation in the control of adult dangerousness. There were 126 juvenile offenders who appeared in court in 1973 on charges of violent crime. We assumed a willingness on the part of the legislature and the judiciary to impose severe incarcerative restraint on all juveniles charged with offenses which would be felonies if committed by adults. We will not let this account of our procedure pass without explicitly saying that neither we nor any other responsible observers we know of believe that a five year sentence of confinement is a fair or appropriate way for the state to respond to delinquency, nor do we suppose that such a policy is likely to convert "bad" boys and girls into good citizens. Throughout this research we have been concerned to discover what we can about the potential value of incapacitation alone in reducing violent crime.

Anyone considering increased use of incarceration for the purpose of reducing crime must respond to the "false-positive" issue, the issue of those who would be incapacitated even though they would not have committed a crime. If we are to restrain offenders because they are identified as dangerous—rather than for their just desert—how much injustice will we do? A criminal record is the best known predictor of future criminal behavior, but it is far from infallible. To lock up a criminal for years, when he might have been given a lesser sanction, simply to prevent him from committing another crime, will result in the needless restraint of men and women who would not in fact commit another crime. To find out the extent of this apparent injustice, we drew a sample of 164 persons arrested for violent offenses in 1966 and traced their criminal histories subsequent to the completion of their sentences to discover how many violent offenses would have been prevented by prolonging the incapacitating term.

The most significant limitation of this battery of studies is obvious. We can only make assertions about known offenders and those offenses that they have been known to commit. Policy-makers cannot concern themselves about disposing of offenders whom the police have not caught. To restrain the unknown offender, he must first be apprehended. The community's only recourse is to allocate more resources to finding and charging more unknown offenders.

But as to the offenses that known offenders have committed but which are either not known to the police or charged by the prosecutor, the situation drifts back into speculation. Some of these divinations are grounded on nothing more than bias, intuition, or simple arithmetic applied to the police statistics. The results are screened through the interpreter's personal version of good common sense. Lately, however, the vogue for self-report studies has seemed to some researchers to offer a more objective foundation for the speculation about the amount of crime which can be prevented by custodial confinement.

Reliance on self-reporting studies imposes difficult, possibly insoluble statistical problems, even if the validity of the method is accepted. Convicts will respond, when asked, to questions about the frequency and nature of their previous crimes, but it cannot be supposed that they represent the universe of criminals, even if their responses can be accepted as accurate. The universe of criminals consists of a variety of humanity that ranges from the once-only offender through intermittent criminals who mix in their occasional crimes with more conventional living, and some who have intensively committed themselves to lifetime criminal careers, never intending to earn an honest living. The distribution within that universe defies sampling; we can be certain that any group questioned will be unrepresentative. No investigator can hope to assign firm values for the distribution of the criminal universe so that he could administer self-reporting questionnaires to credible samples.

Without statistical support, the criminologist must still fall back on speculation as to the value of (λ), the symbol representing the average number of crimes which would be committed yearly by offenders if they were not imprisoned. Conceding that there is no satisfactory solution of this problem, we can make only limited claims for our findings. We do know how much known violent crime might have been prevented by incarceration; we know how many offenders would have been incapacitated by preventive sentencing from the commission of offenses which in fact they did not commit. Most significant of all, we know how many offenses would not have been prevented by incarceration after the commission of a previous offense because the offenders charged in 1973 were "virgins" in crime. Data of these kinds define some of the boundaries for speculation. There remains the value of λ, as to which the policy-maker must consult his conscience. He will also do well to consider the economic consequences of the value he assigns to this coefficient as measured in the number of prison cells needed. As the value of λ increases, the need for longer terms will also increase; the world needs more protection from the high-λ offender than it does from one with a lesser value. But what is certain in this otherwise uncertain world of criminological prediction is that the costs of custody will rise for the predictable future independently of the crime rates and regardless of what is or what is not to be done with those who are incarcerated.

Essentially, the introduction of λ in the criminologist's model building is a speculation about the collective past of a group of criminals with some claim to homogeneity. The ascription of dangerousness is a prediction about the future behavior of such a group. Whether this prediction is derived from the common characteristics of their criminal histories, from actuarial processes, or from clinical study, to say that a criminal is dangerous is to say that there is a serious chance that he will in the future commit a crime of violence. The law makes no provision for the restraint of a citizen on the supposition that he is potentially violent if he has never committed a crime and is not diagnosed as psychotic. To sentence a recidivist to an incapacitating term because of a prediction that falls short of certainty discomfits the libertarian who places a primacy on equality before the law for all citizens. For those who give precedence to crime control and public safety, the prediction that an offender has a 20 to 30 percent chance of committing a violent crime puts him into a special class, different from the rest of his fellows, and justifies his restraint even at the cost of his being a false-positive, a potential classification that cannot be verified if he is incarcerated. Criminologists can agonize over the ethical dilemma, but they cannot resolve it with their empirical methods. They are limited to collecting data, discussing implications, and leaving to the domain of the moralists to carry on the debate over the ethical issues. Considered in the light of the accumulating literature on the incapacitation of criminals, this book will give moralists plenty to think about.

Some may argue along with Sir James Fitzjames Stephen that the incapacitation of dangerous offenders is a moot question. After all, the crimes they commit are at the highest level of gravity and ordinarily to be punished by long incarceration. If a man has committed a crime for which the penalty is ten years in prison, incapacitation will be the by-product of retributive justice. The prediction of dangerousness is of less importance to setting the term of his confinement than is the retributive consideration that actually determined it.

We grant the force of this argument, but the scaling of retributive justice cannot escape the prediction of future violence. A severe sentence will express society's abhorrence of a heinous crime, but its duration may be calculated with an eye on the probability of its repetition. The killer in a crime of passion is a murderer who must be punished by a long sentence to prison, but it will be conceded that he will probably never repeat his offense and can therefore be released as soon as the law is satisfied that its retributive promise has been kept. A contract murderer, the "hit man" of organized crime, is both abhorrent and a probable recidivist of the most serious kind; in his case a conservative prediction must influence a judgment of the appropriate term of incarceration. Between these extremes, violence of many kinds is committed by many different kinds of people, with causes ranging from accident to the most degraded malevolence. Statisticians cannot provide an actuarial base for prediction that improves markedly over the common sense notion that if a man has done it before he is likely to do it again, and much more likely if he has done it twice or more. Our study will represent the consequences of varying sentencing policies based on the common sense that has to stand in the place of prediction by actuaries.

The famous political scientist, James Q. Wilson, has observed that "Wicked people exist. Nothing avails except to set them apart from innocent people."[10] If the restraint of the wicked is to be a primary object of justice, our study will set forth the difficulties of accommodating this objective within the edifice of criminal justice as it now stands. And if, like most human phenomena, wickedness is a relative, changeable characteristic, hard to prove and apt to change with events and circumstances, our data suggest the human cost of assuming that it is an absolute and indelible trait of those to whom it is ascribed.

The Lexicon of Punishment

In a report of this kind certain nouns must be repeated monotonously if rigor of exposition is to be maintained. This introductory chapter is the place to define, once and for all, the essential instruments of our analysis. None of the terms will be unfamiliar to the informed reader, and we do not think that any of our definitions will be seriously controversial. To be sure that we are understood precisely these are the rules of nomenclature to which we will conform.

Punishment is the act of the state of inflicting adverse consequences on a convicted offender. *Nulla poena sine lege*: Punishment is an official act prescribed in the law. In the United States it is limited to death by execution, custodial confinement in some incarcerative facility, surveillance by an official of the state, a fine paid to the state or restitution paid to the victim, and community service orders. The law requires punishment to gain some end, generally giving primacy to retribution, but punishment is not an end in itself.

The objects of punishment are retribution, incapacitation, general deterrence, special deterrence or intimidation, and rehabilitation. We will not review the numerous metamorphoses each of these concepts has undergone since they were first introduced into penal discourse by Jeremy Bentham in the late eighteenth century. Each has been subject to changes in emphasis during the two centuries in which they have been applied, but each must be considered in any discussion of any one of them, if only to be sure that the proper distinctions are made.

Retribution is the consequence of law violation. It fulfills that part of the social contract wherein the citizen yields to the state his right to revenge for wrongs done to him in return for his protection by the state from the dangers inherent in anarchy. It is to be administered so that punishment imposed is proportionate to the crime committed and is therefore sometimes referred to as the "just desert,"[11] inflicted on the offender because it is deemed by some criteria for the classification of crimes that the punishment to which he is sentenced is *deserved*. But it is worth preserving the elasticity of the term *retribution*. Retributive punishment should be, but may not be, a just desert.

Incapacitation is limited to preventing a criminal from committing another offense by executing or incarcerating him. We finesse the commission of crimes in prison so far as this report is concerned; we have considered only those offenses committed in the community. Incapacitation is an absolute; an offender is either incapacitated or he is not. We choose to continue using this term in spite of the objections raised by Wolfgang and Collins,[12] who prefer to use *restraint*, a noun for which we have other uses. The objections made by these authors are based on their understanding that *incapacitation* implies disability, whereas *restraint* "implies hindrance, confinement, abridgement and limitation." Precisely because incapacitation is restricted to disability only, whereas restraint includes various levels of control or attempted control, we shall persist in referring to the incapacitation of offenders when we refer to that object of punitive incarceration. We are fortified in our perseverance by noting how firmly embedded in the language this usage has become; it began with Bentham and has been consistent in its meaning ever since. Terminological changes seldom improve discourse; in this case, the substitution of so inclusive a noun as *restraint* can only confuse both writer and reader by adding uncertainty to the meaning of an essential term.

We repeat that when incapacitation is the object of punishment there is an implicit prediction. In the mind of the decision-maker, there is reason to expect that if the convicted offender is not held in custody he will commit another crime. Therefore the decision to incapacitate is always based on a prediction that is convincing to the person making the decision. In the past the prediction was necessarily intuitive; this continues to be the case today for the most part, despite the zeal of actuarially minded statisticians. Our study is a test of the predictability of a violent offense and a measure of the prevalence of dangerousness, a term that we will define later in this section.

Restraint, as used in our title and throughout our text refers to any intervention, including incarceration, that restricts the freedom of the individual. Surveillance by the police or by a probation officer, week-end incarceration, assignment to a halfway house or group home, or enforced compliance with the conditions of probation or parole all constitute restraint because they interfere with the free movement of the offender. The distinction between incapacitation and restraint is fundamental for this study. We are primarily interested in the extent to which prison terms can reduce crime rates.

General deterrence is the accepted term for the inhibiting effect on potential offenders of the example of punishment inflicted, particularly in the case of crimes that might be chosen by actual or potential offenders. We are not specially concerned with this topic in this study; our methods were not designed to explore the effectiveness of punishment as a general deterrent.

Special deterrence is the effect of punishment in preventing further offenses by the person being punished. The assumption that this process is effective rests on the Utilitarian principle that the experience of punishment is unpleasant enough to induce anyone undergoing it to prefer lawful to unlawful conduct merely to avoid more unpleasant experience. It would be more accurate to refer to special deterrence as *intimidation*, and it will be recalled that in the excerpt from Bentham earlier quoted, this term was used.

Rehabilitation is an omnibus and inaccurate word which includes all benign measures taken by criminal justice officials with the intent of changing the attitude and behavior of criminals so that they will be able to choose lawful means of satisfying their basic needs. Rehabilitative measures are supposed to prevent future crime by providing the power to change; they must be distinguished from the special deterrent effect of punishment, which may have the same result but as a consequence of intimidation rather than redirection. In recent years the concept of rehabilitation has been severely attacked by writers who infer from the ineffectiveness of rehabilitative measures in reducing recidivism that the effort to change offenders is fruitless. Although we disagree with this sweeping conclusion, it must be understood that we can shed no light on the effectiveness of rehabilitation during the period of incapacitation.

To arrive at a meaning for the terms *danger* and *dangerousness* to which we could apply measurements, we had to choose an arbitrary, operational definition. The law cannot take into account a criminal act that has not been committed nor a potential criminal who has not yet violated a law. Therefore, a violent person had to be one who had committed at least one act of violence, but since many crimes of violence are isolated and singular incidents in lives otherwise free of criminality, the dangerous offender was defined as one who had committed two or more crimes of violence. Two terms from the vocabulary of criminal statistics require definition for the general reader. For its statistical classification of crimes, the Federal Bureau of Investigation lists seven offenses as *index* or *Part I* crimes. These crimes are murder and nonnegligent manslaughter, forcible rape, aggravated assault, robbery, burglary, larceny theft, and motor-vehicle theft. The measurement of crime rates is based on the incidence of these offenses as reported by law enforcement agencies throughout the country and compiled in the *Uniform Crime Reports* published annually by the FBI. Although our obvious primary interest is in the four "index crimes of violence," it will be noted that many of the subjects in our study committed one or more of the nonviolent index offenses during the course of their criminal careers.

Some authors add burglary to the four crimes against the person and call the five offenses in the group "safety crimes." We will have occasional use for this term, even though we do not consider burglary a crime of violence for the purpose of this study.

The loose usage of the word *violence* requires tightening. Our decision was to limit the class of violent crimes to the four index crimes, as specified by the Federal Bureau of Investigation. That meant that a number of crimes which might qualify as violent were ruled out, as, for example, assault and battery, a misdemeanor; arson, arguably nonviolent in some situations; sexual molestation and imposition, often if not usually nonviolent in any sense of the word consistent with murder, rape, aggravated assault, and robbery. As to the latter, we had to face the nonviolent, almost ritual quality of some robberies, but we face it in company with the *Uniform Crime Reports* with which we are consistent and can make comparisons where useful or necessary.

To eliminate one source of confusion, we must first deal with the definition of *clearance*, a basic term for subsequent chapters. The distinction between *cleared* and *uncleared* in police usage sets an essential boundary for us. It is used in a somewhat different sense in our analysis, and we will establish the nature of that difference here.

The administrative use of the term is prescribed by the Federal Bureau of Investigation and is followed in principle by the Columbus Police Department. As the FBI defines the term, the requirements for clearance are fairly unambiguous:

> Law enforcement agencies clear a crime when they have identified the offender, have sufficient evidence to charge him, and actually take him into custody. Crime solutions are also recorded in *exceptional instances* [our italics] when some element beyond police control precludes the placing of formal charges against the offender, such as the victim's refusal to prosecute after the offender is identified, or local prosecution is declined because the subject is being prosecuted elsewhere for a crime committed in another jurisdiction. The arrest of one person can clear several crimes[13]

Although this definition is obviously necessary to provide for administrative control of investigations and to monitor the relative success of the police in apprehending offenders and closing investigations, it is too loose for our purposes. We required a datum which allowed a minimum of ambiguity and could provide us with a foundation of certainty. We limited our use of the term to an arrest on record or a conviction on record. We have indicated which kind of clearance we mean whenever there is a possibility of confusion.

The discrepancy between the police data and ours is most apparent in the case of aggravated assault. Our data show that only 13.9 percent of the reported crimes in this category for 1973 were actually cleared, whereas the statistics of the Columbus Police Department show that 89.5 percent of the aggravated assaults reported were cleared.[14] This chasm is readily acceptable but not easily reconciled with the FBI definition quoted above. Assaults are usually committed by persons known to the victim. The injury may be great, but for many reasons the victim will choose not to proceed with charges after the police arrive and place the offender under control. In such cases, the clearance is said to be a clearance by investigation, and it may be seen that this is the case far more frequently than in the "exceptional instances" allowed by the FBI definition. In the same way, but less conspicuously, clearances for forcible rape, as reported by the Columbus police, vary from the clearance figures used in our study. The police cleared 73.9 percent of the rapes reported. Because we must make frequent use of the terms *cleared* and *uncleared* this source of terminological confusion must be kept in mind especially in chapter 6.

These are the terms from the general vernacular of criminology that require some understanding between the reader and ourselves. As our exposition proceeds, terms of art peculiar to this study will make their appearance, and we shall define them as the need arises. Although our procedure is unusual, our concepts are simple and will not strain the bounds of ordinary English usage.

Notes

1. We are not as pessimistic as the authorities usually cited in this connection. Although formal evaluations of rehabilitative programs have been almost universally inconclusive at best, we share the scepticism frequently voiced by Robert Martinson as to the adequacy of research design in the evaluation of correctional programs. See his well-known article, "What Works?—Questions and Answers about Prison Reform," in *The Public Interest*, no. 35 (Spring 1974):22-54, for a brief explication of the massive study reported in Douglas Lipton, Robert Martinson, and Judith Wilks, *The Effectiveness of Correctional Treatment* (New York: Praeger, 1975). A more comprehensive theoretical discussion of the potentiality of correctional treatment, based on an empirical study, is to be found in Gene Kassebaum, David Ward, and Daniel Wilner, *Prison Treatment and Parole Survival* (New York: Wiley, 1971). On the whole, we accept the probability that prison treatment has little, if any effect on the recidivism of released prisoners, but we cannot consider the case closed, especially as to treatment programs where the volition of the prisoner is scrupulously respected, as described in Norval Morris' *The Future of Imprisonment* (Chicago and London: The University of Chicago Press, 1974).

2. The recent publication of Alfred Blumstein, Jacqueline Cohen and Daniel Nagin (Eds), *Deterrence and Incapacitation: Estimating the Effects of Criminal Sanctions on Crime Rates* (Washington, D.C.: National Academy of Sciences, 1978) affords a comprehensive perspective on the present state of thought and the condition of the literature on these topics. For a full review of the contributions of economists to the study of deterrence, see Jan Palmer, "Economic Analysis of the Deterrence Effect of Punishment: A Review," *Journal of Research in Crime and Delinquency*, vol. 14, no. 1 (1977):4-21.

3. The influential work of James Q. Wilson heavily stresses the importance of incapacitation as a means of reducing crime rates. See, for example, *Thinking About Crime* (New York: Basic Books, 1975):172-173: ". . . we would view the correctional system as having a very different function—namely to isolate and to punish . . . it is . . . a recognition that society really does not know how to do much else," and pp. 200-201, where the work of Shlomo and Reuel Shinnar is cited as authority for the estimate that serious crime could be reduced by two-thirds if every person convicted of a serious offense could be imprisoned for three years. The basic assumption permeating the work of Ernest van den Haag is that increased use of imprisonment will proportionately decrease crime rates. See his *Punishing Criminals, Concerning a Very Old and Painful Question* (New York: Basic Books, 1975). While much of his argument is a priori, he draws on the work of Marvin E. Wolfgang, Robert M. Figlio, and Thorsten Sellin *Delinquency in a Birth Cohort* (Chicago and London: The University of Chicago Press, 1972) for authority for the proposition that the incapacitation of a small number of chronic offenders would disproportionately reduce the crime rate. (See pp. 246-250.) But see Blumstein, Cohen, and Nagin, *Deterrence and Incapacitation*, especially pp. 187-237, for a consideration of the present state of knowledge.

4. Wilson, *Thinking About Crime*, 199.

5. Van den Haag, *Punishing Criminals* 242-245. Although this author would give priority to the dangerous offender in providing postpunishment confinement, he argues that there is a case for introducing the practice for nonviolent recidivists, too. He concedes that the confinement should not be punitive, but allows that the effect cannot be altogether removed.

6. Joan Petersilia, Peter W. Greenwood, Marvin Lavin, *Criminal Careers of Habitual Felons* (Santa Monica, Calif.: Rand Corporation, 1977).

7. Jeremy Bentham, *Works* (Bowring Edition, reproduced from volumes published in 1838-1843 by Russell and Russell, New York, 1962), 396.

8. Ibid., 430-431.

9. James Fitzjames Stephen, *History of the Criminal Law of England* (New York: Burt Franklin, 1883), 83.

10. Wilson, *Thinking About Crime*, 209. Compare with Stephen, *Criminal Law of England*, 91: "My own experience is that there are in the world a considerable number of extremely wicked people, disposed, when opportunity offers, to get what they want by force or fraud, with complete indifference to the interests of others, and in ways which are inconsistent with the existence of civilised society. Such persons, I think, ought in extreme cases to be destroyed."

11. Norval Morris discusses the principles of "desert" crisply but without providing guidance on how desert is to be matched with the wrong done in his *The Future of Imprisonment* (Chicago and London: The University of Chicago Press, 1975) 60, 79. There is a tortuous discussion of the topic in Andrew von Hirsch, *Doing Justice* (New York: Hill and Wang, 1976) 45-55. The difficulties

of arriving at guidelines incorporating the idea of just desert are recognized by the author and his colleagues, but it is not clear that they are resolved. For Nigel Walker's thorough critique of this venture into neoclassical criminology, see *British Journal of Criminology*, vol. 18, no. 1 (1977) 79-84. Walker notes that von Hirsch at the outset promises to distinguish between *desert* and *vengeance*, but never gets around to explaining the distinction.

12. Marvin E. Wolfgang and James J. Collins Jr., *Offender Careers and Restraint: Probabilities and Policy Implications* (Unpublished Report prepared at the Center for Studies in Criminology and Criminal Law, University of Pennsylvania, 1977) 5-7.

13. Federal Bureau of Investigation, *Uniform Crime Reports, 1973* (Washington, D.C.: Superintendent of Documents, 6 September 1974), p. 28. There have been slight textual modifications in this definition in subsequent editions of this series, but no apparent change in substance. We use the 1973 definition because it governed the recording of clearances in Columbus during the year under study.

14. Columbus, Ohio, Division of Police, Annual Report 1977, unnumbered table, "Offenses Cleared, 15 Year Summary" 6.

2 Explorations, Speculations, and Models

During the last decade, which saw an upswelling of public anxiety about increasing crime, the application of statistical analysis to the data of criminal justice has risen to a new level of complexity. Eager for innovations that might promise to reduce the social burden of crime, planners and administrators have turned to economists and statistical model builders to increase their understanding of the phenomena they are charged to control. Questions that had hardly been asked in years past were tackled by mathematicians undeterred by the raggedness of the available data, but confident that the deficiencies could and would be corrected once the requirements of the models they constructed were understood. Future crime rates were related to past birth rates and changing economic conditions. The mysteries of general deterrence—the capability of criminal justice to prevent crime by intimidating potential offenders—have begun to yield approximate solutions.[1] A third territory for the statistical pioneer to invade is the power of the system to reduce crime by incapacitating various classes of offenders. As will be obvious to the reader of the concluding chapter of this book, we are the beneficiaries of these earlier explorers.

Although some relatively abstruse studies of the potential effects of an incapacitation policy had been completed as early as 1972, interest among policy-makers became widespread only with the publication in 1975 of the influential essays of James Q. Wilson,[2] a political scientist, and Ernest van den Haag,[3] a social philosopher. Their views gained the attention of a president,[4] and struck a theme of severity as a remedy for crime which has reverberated throughout the country.

Because the roughly similar views of these authors drew on some of the mathematical assessments of incapacitation that we will discuss in this chapter, it is appropriate to review their positions before proceeding to a discussion of the models of restraint with which we are concerned in this chapter. Both authors share the conception that there exists an operational policy that gives primacy to the rehabilitation of the offender—a notion for which there is no evidence except a mass of wishful but unfulfilled thinking.[5] Both of them take pains to show that it is vain to expect that offenders can be rehabilitated at the behest of authority and unjust to relate the duration of a prison term to the success of rehabilitation. Each considered what else the criminal justice system might do to prevent or diminish the incidence of crime. One strategy that looked promising was a uniform policy of incapacitation. Citing studies that show that most serious crime is committed by repeaters, Wilson thought that the proper function of the correction system should be to: "... isolate and punish. It is a measure of our confusion that such a statement will strike many enlightened readers today as cruel, even barbaric. It is not. It is merely a recognition that society ... must be able to protect itself from dangerous offenders ... it is also a frank admission that society really does not know how to do much else."[6]

Wilson's surmise about the potential crime reduction to be achieved by incapacitation is formulated in this passage:

> The purpose of isolating ... offenders is obvious: Whatever they may do when they are released, they cannot harm society while confined or closely supervised. The gains from merely incapacitating convicted criminals may be very large. If much or most serious crime is committed by repeaters, separating repeaters from the rest of society, even for relatively brief periods of time, may produce major reductions in crime rates.[7]

For an estimate of how great these reductions might be, Wilson appealed to the work of Shlomo and Reuel Shinnar, who had produced a paper in which the claim was made that mandatory sentences of five years for crimes against the person and three years for burglary would reduce the incidence of these offenses by as much as two-thirds. (Later in this chapter, we shall summarize the Shinnars' seminal research. Here we are interested in their influence on one of the most influential contemporary writers on criminal justice.) Wilson was cautious enough to allow that even if the Shinnars' estimates were over-stated by a factor of two, serious crime would be reduced by a third, not an inconsiderable gain.[8]

The retributivist philosophy expounded by van den Haag is basic to his proposals for the restoration of order. Only when the threat of punishment is credible because it is inflicted on the guilty does retribution perform its proper function by setting the boundaries of acceptable behavior. But van den Haag observes that punishment is useful beyond the performance of this moral obligation: it controls crime "... in three additional ways: (1) by incapacitating offenders, (2) by reforming them through intimidation or rehabilitation, and (3) by deterring others from committing offenses."[9] Van den Haag's argument with regard to reformation and deterrence is familiar and need not detain us here. As to incapacitation, though, this author concedes its limitations:

> ... incapacitation does not decrease the offenses of convicts who would not have committed additional offenses anyway—e.g., of generally lawabiding citizens who committed a "crime of passion" in a specific, nonrecurrent situation. ...

> Whatever the effects of incapacitation on the number of crimes a prisoner commits over his lifetime, they must not be confused with effects on the crime rate ... the temporary or even permanent incapaci-

tation of convicts reduces the crime rate only if there is no compensating increase of crime by others. Often there is.[10]

Van den Haag then adopts some similes from the storehouse of elementary economics to show that "the total number of persons engaged in producing shoes or crimes soon adjusts to produce the output determined by profitability. Incapacitation is effective mainly when the forces that determine the production of crime cannot be compared with the forces that determine the supply of shoes."[11]

He does not seem to have known about the Shinnars' study of incapacitation as a means of reducing the number of violent or "safety" crimes (homicide, rape, felonious assault, robbery, and burglary), and therefore was not beguiled into the expectation that increased severity will reduce their incidence. On the contrary, he seems to suppose that such a policy will have little effect on the crime rates, but can be justified as a measure of protection to society. In making this argument he relies heavily on the study of the Philadelphia birth cohort by Marvin Wolfgang and colleagues. This massive research came to many conclusions, but none so famous as the finding that a very small number of boys in the cohort—about 6 percent—committed most of the serious crimes. These individuals were defined as those who committed five or more offenses before they were eighteen, and were designated by the Wolfgang group as *chronic offenders*. Van den Haag was impressed by this finding and its implications. Uneasily but clearly, he proposed an innovation: For the chronic recidivist there must be "post-punishment incapacitation," based on a reasonable prediction from the past behavior of the offender that he will offend again. Van den Haag was unwilling to indicate the duration of the incapacitation and conceded that it will not be seen by the offender himself as different from punishment. He makes no estimate of the reduction in the crime rate to be expected by this innovation, but concludes that Wolfgang and associates have made a convincing case that chronic offenders commit a disproportionately large number of crimes, and that they can be identified as a group with enough reliability to justify special treatment of the kind he had in mind.

This position accepts the propriety of incapacitation as a policy, but it differs significantly from Wilson's optimism about its effectiveness in reducing crime rates. Based on the Shinnars' model, Wilson's policy, if put into effect, would apply a long prison sentence to certain classes of offenders in the expectation that their removal would reduce the number of people disposed to commit those crimes. Van den Haag is not so sanguine. His bleak view of human nature leads him to the belief that there are more murderers, muggers, and rapists to replace those that are taken into custody. For him incapacitation is justified by the protection it affords the public from known dangers. The possibility that the rates of violent crime will be favorably affected is a welcome contingency, but not to be counted on.

The Conceptual Revival

Although Wilson and van den Haag are entitled to credit for the popularization of the idea of incapacitation as a primary objective of criminal justice, they both leaned on empiricists for support. The most prominent of their conceptual sources were Wolfgang and his associates at the University of Pennsylvania, on whom both writers relied, and the Shinnars, who led Wilson to the surmise outlined above. We begin our review of the small but influential literature on the mathematics of incapacitation with the relevant conclusions of these authors. It will be seen that they have been followed by other investigators who have come to differing conclusions. Nevertheless, all of them have been asking one or the other of two fundamental questions: (1) How many crimes are prevented by the incarceration of certain offenders actually serving sentences? and (2) How many crimes would be prevented by the incarceration of certain classes of offenders who were not in fact incarcerated?

The Wolfgang study of the Philadelphia birth cohort provided both Wilson and van den Haag with a target, a small fraction of the humanity studied which was responsible for the majority of the serious offenses. Following Wolfgang, both these authors concluded that if this fraction of apparently identifiable young men could be taken into protracted custody the streets of Philadelphia would be much safer.

We shall not attempt a complete review of this famous research; the reader who is unfamiliar with its methodology and conclusions should go to the source. However, it is important in this perspective to identify the target of chronic offenders and provide some particulars about its characteristics. The cohort studied by Wolfgang consisted of all males born in 1945 who resided in Philadelphia at least from their tenth until their eighteenth birthday. There were 9,945 of them. Records of police contacts were found for 3,475 in this group, and 627 of these delinquents had five or more such contacts and were therefore designated as *chronic offenders*.[12] This group has become famous. The analysis of the data presented in the original report showed that they were responsible for more than half the total number of offenses committed by all the delinquents and a disproportionate number of the serious offenses. The social and demographic characteristics of the chronic offenders were faithfully tabulated so far as they were available. The probability that any offender, having commited one offense would commit another was calculated for every point in the open-ended continuum of recidivism. The percentage of offenders repeating after the third offense rose to more than 70 percent, and the seriousness of the offenses committed increased as the individual progressed in recidivism.

This finding prompted many writers to conclude that custodial intervention for the chronic offender would be a practical expedient for dramatically reducing the incidence of street crime. The problem was to identify these individuals soon enough to prevent them from committing avoidable crimes. We have seen that van den Haag was attracted by the idea and convinced that it is practical and appropriate. Two questions lurk unanswered in the background:

1. How many boys would have to be locked up to incapacitate the chronic offenders? Six percent of the boys between ten and eighteen in Philadelphia would constitute a considerable group, even if not all of them were locked up at the same time. The three or five year terms proposed by Wilson would create a barely manageable escalation in the size of the juvenile population to be held in custody. If each of the birth cohorts in the mid-1940s produced chronic recidivists at the same rate as the cohort of 1945, three year terms for all these young people would eventually accumulate to an increase of nearly 1,900 in custodial control from Philadelphia alone, disregarding the commitments from the same category from the rest of Pennsylvania, and disregarding all offenders who had not yet achieved chronic status. Whether such an increase in economic and social cost would be acceptable to the people of the state, regardless of the question of feasibility, would be open to serious question.

2. The juxtaposition of an apparently insignificant fraction of all the boys in town with the majority of offenses committed creates a formidable impression when first brought to the attention of a layman. The answer to the crime problem is at hand; lock these people up and transform the quality of urban life. It is not that simple. The Philadelphia birth cohort study was not designed to produce an estimate of the potential reduction of the total volume of crime in the city by a policy of incapacitation. As we shall see, further statistical analysis has been undertaken by two members of the group, leading to estimates of the potential reduction of crime by incarcerating chronic juvenile recidivists. Both studies arrive at an estimated impact on the crime rate far below the hasty inferences of casual readers. As found in *The Violent Few*, an earlier publication of the Dangerous Offender Project,[13] the number of chronic youthful offenders who repeat violent offenses is small indeed. A large percentage of the Columbus cohort committed one offense only, and the chronic recidivists achieved their status by nonviolent offenses added to one or two crimes of violence. We cannot estimate how much serious crime would be prevented by adopting "post-punishment incapacitation" to chronic offenders as defined by Wolfgang, but the reduction would certainly not be in the order of 6 percent.

Our scepticism about the notion that custodial management of chronic offenders should not be taken as a derogation of the enormous value of the Wolfgang study. Certainly these authors have defined a problem to be addressed by social inventors. Like good public policy-makers, they advise a modification of the system aimed at "intervention" in the case of a specific class of recidivist. Cautiously, they avoid specifying the intervention most likely to deal with the conditions these young offenders present, and they scrupulously avoid recommending incarceration. It is gratifying to note that this study has inspired other specific alternatives, as for example the Unified Delinquency Intervention Services (UDIS) in Illinois, designed to provide realistic intervention for chronic inner city recidivists in Chicago.[14] The success of this venture has yet to be settled; whatever the outcome of its evaluation, it avoids the stacking of thousands of boys in large youth facilities, while at the same time it provides significant programs for controlling and helping the chronic delinquent.

The contribution of the Shinnars is a mathematical treatment of available data on crime in New York City designed to set a figure on the extent to which the rate of safety crimes can be reduced by rigorous application of policies of incapacitation.[15] Because of the great influence this technical article has exerted, we will discuss its reasoning and conclusion in some detail.

The authors open their analysis by noting that the huge growth in crime over the previous thirty years had been accompanied by changing patterns of crime control. Risks to a criminal when committing a crime had been greatly reduced. Although the idea of risk is related to the concept of general deterrence, it can be defined as "the average time a criminal can expect to spend in prison per crime committed." This operational definition is used to assess the effect of incapacitation on the rate of safety crimes. On this basis, the Shinnars developed a mathematical model by which this assessment can proceed. The essential elements of the model are the average number of crimes committed in a year, by any given criminal, his likelihood of being caught and imprisoned, and the duration of his incarceration.

The model rests on a series of assumptions:

1. There is a class of criminals that has a high rate of recidivism.

2. This class is responsible for a high fraction of the total crimes committed. (Supporting these assumptions are studies that show that a large fraction of all arrestees are recidivists, and other studies that show that 60-80 percent of offenders recidivate within three or four years.)

3. Each recidivist is responsible for at least five or six crimes per year. (Turning to *Uniform Crime Reports*, they find that the average number of arrests for recidivists is about one per year, but, as only 15-20 percent of index crime is cleared each year, it follows that recidivists average five-six offenses per year.)

4. The true range of actual crimes committed per year per recidivist is six-fourteen.

5. Recidivists must commit most of the 70 percent of crimes that are never cleared by an arrest. (The distribution of arrested offenders according to status as to recidivism will be correct for the uncleared offenders. No other explanation is reasonable. If amateur offenders commit that volume of crime they would have to commit it at a rate of five crimes per male New Yorker, obviously impossible. Nor is it conceivable that there are a large number of professional criminals who are so proficient that they *never* are caught. "If . . . we assume that most unsolved crimes are committed by the same recidivist population

which commits the solved crimes, we come up with a figure of six-[fourteen] crimes per year, while getting caught once, which seems more reasonable."[16])

To account for the apparent rise in the rate of safety crime the Shinnars develop an equation for calculating the effectiveness of the criminal justice system using the total number of index crimes, the number of prisoners, the number of commitments, the average stay in prison, and the chance of conviction for each person committing a safety crime. This equation yields an index of effectiveness which declined from a value of 75-85 percent in 1940 to 56 percent in 1960, and in 1970 it was 20 percent "and fast approaching zero." From this application of their model to the available data, the Shinnars concluded that the vertiginous rise in the rate of safety crime must be attributed to a corresponding collapse in the efficiency of the criminal justice system, as measured by the likelihood of being caught, convicted, and sentenced to an extended term of incarceration.

The Shinnars seized on this complex variable as the element in the equation that could be successfully manipulated to increase personal safety in New York City. If the inconsistent administration of short prison sentences could be altered in favor of mandatory five-year terms for all those who commit violent crimes and three-year terms for all burglars, the street crime situation in the city could be dramatically changed for the better. The basis for their claim was that under the circumstances prevailing at the time of their study, the chance of a mugger being arrested for any given mugging was 12 percent; the chance of imprisonment after arrest was 10 percent; therefore the chance of a mugger being so unlucky as to be actually incarcerated was about 1.2 percent. But if every convicted mugger were to be sent to prison for five years, the volume of mugging would be reduced by a factor of five, remembering that it was assumed in the model that each arrested mugger had committed from six to fourteen muggings during each year that he was not arrested.

The Shinnars estimated that the total prison population of New York state would increase by about 20,000—"substantial but not extreme."[17] They added that this policy would have a deterrent effect and once implemented, recruits to violent crime would diminish in number. Their arithmetic was based on misinformation. The total capacity of the prisons in New York City and New York State at that time was between 17,000 and 20,000 (prison capacity being a flexible parameter at best), whereas their projection was for a total population of between 40,000 and 60,000 to be incarcerated for safety crimes alone if their suggested policy were adopted.

The mathematics of the Shinnars' model are worth some explication here; the remaining models to be considered have a family resemblance to the formulas created by these investigators and can share the same notation. They begin with the notion that they can estimate the time available to a career criminal to commit crimes by solving the equation:

$$\frac{\text{Average time between commitments}}{\text{Average time between commitments + average time in prison}} = \frac{\frac{1}{\lambda q J}}{\frac{1}{\lambda q^J} + S}$$

where λ = crime rate per year per criminal;   (2.1)

   q = probability of getting convicted, having committed a crime, before he commits another crime;

   J = probability of being committed to jail, having been convicted of a crime;

   S = length of sentence, exponentially distributed with mean S.

The left side of the equation, a fraction representing the time free to commit crimes divided by the average length of a criminal career, including time incapacitated, is obvious enough. On the right side are the basic ingredients of a criminal justice policy, all of which, it is presumed, can be varied by official action. It follows that the average time between commitments depends on varying the probability of a jail sentence and the length of the sentence imposed.

The Shinnars then proceed to a statement of the ratio of crimes to be committed under any given official policy to those to be committed under no policy at all. This ratio is expressed as follows:

$$\frac{\text{E}(x) \text{ at a given } qJS}{\text{E}(x) \text{ of } qJS \text{ equal to zero}} = \frac{\lambda T/(1 + \lambda q JS)}{\lambda T} = \frac{1}{1 + \lambda q JS} \qquad (2.2)$$

where $\text{E}(x)$ = expected value of x, the number of crimes a criminal commits

   T = average length of a criminal career.

This model is an elaborate basis for calculating the varying effects of differing criminal justice policies on the crime rates. Some of the estimates on which the model must depend can never be refined to exact values; they must forever remain estimates. The average length of different kinds of criminal careers, the number of crimes a criminal may commit, and the crime rate for any time period are values that will be influenced by even more shadowy variables, for example, economic conditions, social dislocations, and the general perceptions of legitimate opportunities as compared with criminal opportunities. In the Shinnars' model, the range allowed for λ (six-fourteen crimes per year) obviously results in considerable variance in the values for $\text{E}(x)$, wholly apart from the many other influences on crime conditions that the model cannot take into consideration.

Nevertheless, the model provides a demonstration of the effects of increased police efficiency, increased severity in the courts, and increased jail time in modifying crime rates. The central assumption is that there exists a population of recidivist criminals who, if restrained by incarceration, would be unable to commit the very large fraction of the total number of violent crimes committed for which they are responsible. Our account of the Shinnars' mathematics is necessarily abbreviated. They have raised a significant question in their study and in the interesting demonstration at which they arrived.

The merits of this model deserve specific comment. First, it allows the statistician an opportunity to estimate the effects of differing policies of incapacitation. Second, the impact of parameter perturbation (q, J, and S) on the crime rate can be isolated for comparisons. Finally, the model can be used to estimate shifts in the prison population as a result of changes in criminal justice policy.

Its main weakness is its dependence of definite values for such entities as λ, which can never be more than roughly estimated. Whatever value is assigned to this variable, alternative values can be justified with equal plausibility which would significantly alter the projections obtained.

In her critique of the Shinnars' model, Jacqueline Cohen has added two more reservations.[18] First, these authors have not allowed for the constraints on the system imposed by overloading. The likelihood of imprisonment is not a policy choice. Where there is insufficient prosecutorial and judicial time, prosecutors will resort to plea bargaining, thereby compromising any fidelity to the strict policy suggested by the Shinnars. The prosecutorial overload in New York City has been notoriously subject to this kind of adjustment. It must be added that a comparable effect of overloading works on the police, who can arrest and report and present testimony in only a finite number of cases during any given period. We do not agree that this consideration is an objection to the validity of the model; indeed, this reality serves to explain the decline in the effectiveness of the system that was demonstrated by the Shinnars.

Cohen also shows that the Shinnars are far too optimistic about the increase in the prison population that would result from the application of the policy they propose. She points out that the 1970 prison population of New York State consisted of 9,000 felons committed for safety crimes as part of the 12,500 for all felonies. It is clear that this increase, if limited to these estimates, would result in a prison population amounting to about 25 percent of the total population of all the prisons in the United States during that year. It would be an increase of between 355 and 567 percent in the New York prison population alone.

The usefulness of the Shinnars' model is limited to its pioneering application of statistical techniques to the estimate of the incapacitative effects of incarcerative control of violent offenders. The rigor of the model does not and probably cannot correspond to the necessary vagaries of a system that must allow for discretion in its application of policy. The law can and sometimes does require the court to impose flat mandatory sentences for certain serious offenses. So far, it has not succeeded in limiting the discretion of the police officer making an arrest or the prosecutor in negotiating charges and pleas. If statistical equations can be formulated to allow for these ineradicable elements of decision-making in criminal justice, the supporting logic is certainly not yet in sight.

But although the construction of such a model is an achievement not to be denigrated, the Shinnars did not take into account some of the available statistics that could have increased confidence in their conclusions. We have already mentioned Cohen's assessment of the discrepancy between their estimate of the increase of the New York prison population and the minimum increase to be expected. Their opinion that murder and felonious assault are "mostly committed by career criminals (65 percent in New York City, 70 percent in the FBI study)" is beyond accounting.[19] They have apparently inferred from the data of the *National Prisoner Statistics* that most persons incarcerated for assault are recidivists, overlooking the fact that the persons convicted of that offense constitute a minority of those who commit it. Nor does the *National Prisoner Statistics* series attempt to distinguish career criminals from incidental offenders; the data collected are sparse and crude, certainly insufficient to warrant a conclusion so much at variance with what is known of the data of homicide and assault.

The creation of the Shinnar model, then, is an achievement which has been marred by special pleading. A well-conceived supporting logic has been used to advocate a policy of rigorous incapacitation without testing the results against data that could have been collected and analyzed. That two policy analysts could have undertaken such an exercise is understandable; that social scientists with more experience with the system should take it seriously enough to use in arguing for new policy is a puzzling lapse of responsibility.

Other Explorations

An interesting variation on the Shinnar model can be found in the work of David Greenberg.[20] Relying principally on California data, Greenberg estimated that each one-year reduction in average sentence length would result in increases in the index crime rates of from 1.2 to 8.0 percent. This study rests on debatable assumptions. Greenberg estimates that the true figure for return to prison with convictions for new crimes during the first year after release will approximate 8 percent, a much lower figure than usually suggested. The discrepancy is attributable to the exclusion of technical parole violations. Greenberg finally arrives at an average rate of index crimes committed by recidivists within a range of 0.5 to 4.3 crimes per recidivist per year. His calculation also rests on the dubious assumption that the average duration of a criminal career is five years, arguing that the higher averages usually accepted underrepresent one-crime offenders. He also inflates the crime rates reported in the *Uniform Crime Reports* by a multiplier derived from victimization studies. Greenberg's analysis concludes with two important and credible speculations. First, the low level of incapacitation which he infers from the data is attributable in part to the low rate of commission of serious crime by parolees. His second speculation points to the low rate of incarceration for index crimes. Obviously, if a more severe policy of restraint were applied, the incapacitative effects of imprisonment would substantially increase.

Cohen believes that Greenberg's estimates of the impact of incapacitation are too low. This is so because his estimates of λ are not adjusted to compensate for the length of time a recidivist is incarcerated. If, for example, an offender committed three crimes in a year, but spent half that year in prison, the offender was actually committing crimes at the rate of six per year. Despite this problem of calculating λ on calendar rather than street time, Cohen suggests that Greenberg's conclusion is realistic. Incapacitation, as presently imposed, does not prevent much crime.[21]

One of the earliest economists to engage in studies of deterrence and incapacitation was Isaac Ehrlich, whose disquisition, "Participation in Illegitimate Activities" appeared in 1972.[22] Ehrlich's reasoning led him to the conclusion that deterrence was about ten times more influential than incapacitation in accounting for changes in the crime rates. His mathematics indicates that when incarceration is a sanction, its imposition results in two distinguishable effects on the crime rate. Increased risk of a more severe sentence will deter potential offenders, whereas their separation from society will prevent them from committing crimes that they would otherwise be free to perpetrate.

In her critique of studies of incapacitation, Cohen questions the reasoning by which Ehrlich arrived at the value of λ. His calculation of the total effect of imprisonment assumes that its impact on the crime rate can be limited to the respective influences of incapacitation and deterrence as represented by coefficients chosen for these variables. His choice of a value for λ is improbably low—one crime per offender. But if the value of λ is increased, the coefficient for deterrence must decrease. The more crimes an offender commits, the less he is deterred by the system from committing them. In view of the improbability that λ is equal to unity in New York City or any other metropolitan center with a high crime rate, it seems certain that Ehrlich has seriously underestimated the overall effectiveness of incapacitation and overestimated the effect of deterrence.

Despite his reliance on assumptions that cannot be supported by evidence, Ehrlich has performed a considerable service to the understanding of the interaction between the criminal justice system and the crime rate. If the crime rate is seen as the dependent variable, it is affected by two, and only two, influences that the criminal justice system can bring to bear—incapacitation and deterrence. These influences must be covariants. Whether the effectiveness of general deterrence can ever be measured with confidence, its reciprocal relationship with incapacitation is evident in Ehrlich's analysis. Where λ is high, criminals have confidence that the risks imposed by the system are low and therefore believe they can commit crimes with increased impunity. Where λ is low, it must be assumed that criminals have come to an opposite conclusion: The risks are unacceptable. But both values are subject to speculation. Their combined effect on the crime rate will also covary with environmental influences—economic conditions, the cultural sanctions for the use of narcotics, the relative hardness of crime targets. None of these influences are well enough understood to permit the assignment of values in equations. Although we do not foresee a methodology that will make possible such equations to the extent that policy decisions can be confidently made, Ehrlich's mathematics are a useful aid to thought about the relationship that exist among the factors increasing or diminishing the crime rate.

Less familiar than Ehrlich's equations of deterrence and incapacitation is the simple but ingenious model of incapacitation created by Jeffrey Marsh and Max Singer of the Hudson Institute.[23] Acutely aware of imprecision of criminal statistics, they engaged in a thought experiment, using what can be conjectured about the rates of robbery in New York City. Building on a figure of 70,000 robberies reported in New York City in 1970, they decided that probably about 200,000 robberies actually occurred during that year. There were about 3,300 convictions for robbery, but of course there were some robbers who were allowed to plead to lesser offenses. The question to be explored was the effect of a one-year prison sentence for each conviction on the volume of robbery in the city.

The model chosen was based on the plausible notion that robbers differ widely in their proficiency and their commitment to their occupation. Some may be assumed to commit one robbery a year—others may commit as many as 250. The supposition continues that the city's population of robbers can be divided into six groups, each averaging significantly different rates: one, five, ten, fifty, 100, and 250 robberies per year. It was further assumed that the probability of apprehension and conviction would vary considerably from group to group. The groups with highest average frequency will have a lower probability of arrest and conviction, but it is also assumed that the probability of arrest and conviction does not decrease as rapidly as the frequency of robberies increases.

Using this model, the authors arrive at different λ's for each of the six groups. Their reasoning is that there will be a pronounced tendency for high-frequency robbers to accumulate in jail because, although their chance of being caught on any one robbery is small, the number of exposures per year is high, and over time, their probability of arrest and conviction must be higher than for the low-frequency robber. Based on this supposition, it follows that the incapacitative effect of a year of incarceration will be understated if it is based on the average number of robberies for each robber at large. It also follows that in the Marsh-Singer model it can be expected that each year a robber spends in prison will prevent about thirty robberies.

But this is a "thought experiment," principally useful for calling our attention to the diversity of criminal behavior, even among the members of one category of offender. The estimate that the number of robberies might be reduced by from 35 to 48 percent depends on the unsupported assertion that there were in all as many as 200,000 robberies in New York City in 1970. Although that estimate is carefully hedged as lacking in "rigorous foundation," it leads to an argument that much more severe disposition should be provided for. As we shall see, the analysis of the data we have accumulated for Columbus in 1973 bears no resemblance at all to the assumptions made by these writers. The distribution of the reported robberies among the known robbers could not possibly approach the rates that Marsh and Singer thought reasonable but "outrageous."

Further Implications of the Philadelphia Birth Cohort Study

Two authors have drawn conclusions about the incapactitative power of the system from the information accumulated about the Philadelphia birth cohort. Stevens Clarke, the first writer to explore the data in search of an answer to this question, estimated the amount of crime actually prevented by incapacitation. There were 381 boys in the cohort who were locked up for varying periods of time during their juvenile careers. Based on their reported arrests, he calculated an average number of index crimes, year by year, in other words, at ages eleven, twelve, thirteen, and so on. These calculations were performed separately for whites and nonwhites. For each year, he determined how many boys were incarcerated and how much crime was committed by each age group not incarcerated, thereby arriving at an average number of offenses per boy. Multiplying that average by the number of boys incarcerated, Clarke obtained a value for the number of crimes prevented by incarceration. Comparing that sum to the juvenile crime rate, he arrived at an estimate of a crime reduction by incapacitation of between 5 and 15 percent. If it is acceptable to estimate the juvenile share of the Part I offenses at 28 percent, then the incapacitation of juveniles reduced the Philadelphia crime rate by 1 to 4 percent. His conclusion was:

> The results of this analysis also have implications for a law enforcement strategy based on the removal effect as far as juvenile offenders are concerned. Even if it were possible to double the numbers of juvenile

offenders incarcerated, the above figures suggest that the resulting decrease in nationwide index offenses would be only 1 to 4 percent. Considering the problems involved, the benefit is not worth the cost.[24]

In her analysis of the Clarke study, Cohen challenges two assumptions. First, she notes that Clarke implicitly assumed that all boys who were incarcerated had begun a full and active criminal career at about age eight. This appears to be very unlikely. As a result, when Clarke calculates the mean rate of offenses committed at each age, his denominator is greatly expanded, lowering the average rate considerably. Cohen recalculates the average rate by gradually increasing the number of youths committing crime at each age, that is, gradually increasing the denominator. By doing this, the average rate is larger; similarly, the number of crimes prevented by incapacitation is increased.

The second challenge goes to the assumption that the juvenile share of the index offense crime rate is about 28 percent, whereas the FBI data report that 45 percent of the arrestees for these offenses are juvenile. Clarke justified his reduction of that figure by the supposition that juveniles are more likely to be arrested than adults, a notion for which there is no available empirical evidence. Recalculating Clarke's data in the light of her reservations, Cohen estimates that the true reduction of index crime through incapacitation of the 381 juvenile offenders was of the order of 7 to 14 percent.[25]

The second study based on the Philadelphia cohort was conducted by Wolfgang and Collins as a phase of a continuing study of the cohort of 1945.[26] Taking a 10 percent sample (n = 971) of the 9,945 person cohort, records were kept to the thirtieth birthday, and 564 members (58 percent) were interviewed about their criminal activity up to the age of twenty-five. Probably the most remarkable finding was the extent of involvement in crime; by age thirty nearly half the study population, 47 percent, had at least one nontraffic contact with the police. Further, the chronic offenders, those with five or more contacts, comprised 14 percent of the population.

On examining patterns of criminal activity, Wolfgang and Collins found that although the younger offenders committed many more offenses, the offenses committed as they grew older were much more serious. That finding prompted the authors to suggest that policy-makers may prefer to prevent fewer but more serious offenses by more rigorous restraint of adult offenders. Certainly, they affirm, the focus of imprisonment policy should be on chronic offenders; it is calculated that for each chronic offender incarcerated for a year, 2.4 index offenses will be prevented, although many of these offenses would be crimes never reported to the authorities. A second estimate is that for the year 1974, and extrapolating from the records of the 1945 birth cohort, 1,178 index offenses were prevented by the incarceration of male offenders between the ages of fifteen and thirty, thereby reducing the Philadelphia crime rate by 2 percent. "Many more than 1,178 index offenses were prevented by the incarceration of offenders, but only this number of official offenses was prevented."[27] Using the formula developed by the Shinnars, this estimate of prevention is accounted for by the low rate of apprehension by the police and the lower rate of incarceration imposed by the courts.

The policy recommendation emerging from this research is cautious. The authors note that their findings show that for each index offender incarcerated in the fourteen to seventeen age span four to five index offenses would be prevented. For each adult offender incarcerated for a year between the ages of eighteen and twenty-five "roughly three to three-and-a-half index offenses will be prevented."[28] But for chronic offenders of all ages, two and one-half offenses per year will be prevented. Even if focused on these offenders, incapacitation offers little potential for reducing crime. There are simply too many offenders to affect the crime rate by concentrating on one small subset of the criminal population.

Our brief review of the limited literature on the effects of incapacitation is not intended to compete with Cohen's exhaustive exegesis, to which the reader is unhesitatingly referred. It will be seen that the tools are few and the conclusions are widely divergent. Speculation is inevitable, no matter what methods are used, and those that we have adopted have not eliminated that necessity. The tools are familiar. An estimate must be made of qJS, the likelihood of arrest and conviction. Another estimate must be made of λ, the average number of crimes committed by an offender population while at large. Both of these estimates can be grounded in criminal statistics. The central problem is to bound the estimate. It will be seen that the assumptions made by the investigators have resulted in varying conclusions, despite the fairly standard structure of the model with which they have been working.

Referring again to Cohen's definitive review of the literature, there appears to be a convergence on an estimate that the reduction in crime attributable to incapacitation is probably about one quarter of the crimes committed in a given year.[29] That conclusion is consonant with our findings. However, as Cohen also shows, the reduction is likely to be greatest in cities and states with the gravest crime problems. An incapacitation policy in Idaho is going to be much more effective and less costly than the same policy applied in New York's South Bronx. The greater the density of felony offenders—first, multiple, or chronic— the more costly and the less probable is it that this strategy will have the desired crime reduction impact. Cruelly, areas least affected by the reality of crime will benefit most; areas most in need of reduction, least. As an answer for the woes of New York City incapacitation is a flawed approach. As a response to Boise's crime problem, a case of overkill.

Notes

1. For an excellent summary of the state of the art in the application of statistical techniques to the problems of general deterrence and incapacitation, the reader is referred to Alfred Blumstein, Jacqueline Cohen, and Daniel Nagin

(eds.), *Deterrence and Incapacitation: Estimating the Effects of Criminal Sanctions on Crime Rates* (Washington, D.C.: The National Academy of Sciences, 1978). See also, Jan Palmer, "Economic Analyses of the Deterrent Effect of Punishment," *Journal of Research in Crime and Delinquency*, vol. 14, no. 1 (1977):4-21.

2. James Q. Wilson, *Thinking About Crime* (New York: Basic Books, 1975).

3. Ernest van den Haag, *Punishing Criminals* (New York: Basic Books, 1975).

4. President Gerald Ford, *Remarks of the President at the Yale Sesquicentennial Convocation Dinner* (1975).

5. This unconventional position may require some discussion, although it is not germane to the problem of incapacitation. The nation at large has been subjected to a standard discussion of the aims of the criminal justice system in general and the penal system in particular that holds that rehabilitation is a primary goal of the administration of justice. Whether it should be or not may be still open to question. The actuality is that few if any decisions are made with respect to the disposition of individual offenders with any emphasis at all on the prospect of rehabilitation or its achievement. Judges and parole boards have consistently determined sentences by an estimate of the severity of the offense and the risk that it will be committed again by the same offender. For a convincing demonstration of this proposition, see Don Gottfredson, Leslie T. Wilkins, and Peter B. Hoffman, *Guidelines for Sentencing and Parole* (Lexington, Mass.: Lexington Books, 1978).

6. Wilson, *Thinking About Crime* 172-173.

7. Ibid., 173.

8. Ibid., 201.

9. Van den Haag, *Punishing Criminals* 50.

10. Ibid., 51.

11. Ibid., 53.

12. Marvin E. Wolfgang, Robert N. Figlio, and Thorsten Sellin, *Delinquency in a Birth Cohort* (Chicago and London: The University of Chicago Press, 1972). For a general discussion of the *chronic offender*, the fundamental idea so far as this study is concerned, see particularly pp. 88-105, and 248.

13. Donna Martin Hamparian, Richard Schuster, Simon Dinitz, and John P. Conrad, *The Violent Few* (Lexington, Mass.: Lexington Books, D.C. Heath, 1978) 130.

14. For an account of the program, see Charles A. Murray, Doug Thomson, and Cindy B. Israel, *UDIS: Deinstitutionalizing the Chronic Juvenile Offender* (Washington, D.C.: American Institutes for Research, 1978) 43-120. The remainder of this document is an evaluation that remains in question at the time of this writing.

15. Reuel Shinnar and Shlomo Shinnar, "The Effects of the Criminal

Justice System on the Control of Crime," *Law and Society Review*, vol. 9, no. 4 (1975):581-611.

16. Ibid., 598.

17. Ibid., 606.

18. Jacqueline Cohen, "The Incapacitative Effect of Imprisonment: A Critical Review of the Literature" in Blumstein, Cohen, and Nagin (eds.), *Deterrence and Incapacitation* 216-217.

19. Shinnar and Shinnar, "The Effects of the Criminal Justice System" 599.

20. David F. Greenberg, "The Incapacitative Effects of Imprisonment: Some Estimates," *Law and Society Review*, no. 9 1975:541.

21. Jacqueline Cohen, "The Incapacitative Effect" 203-204.

22. Isaac Ehrlich, "Participation in Illegitimate Activities: An Economic Analysis," *Journal of Political Economy*, vol. 81, no. 3 (1974):521-567.

23. Jeffrey Marsh and Max Singer, *Soft Statistics and Hard Questions* (The Hudson Institute, Discussion Paper HI-1712-DP, 1972).

24. Stevens H. Clarke, "Getting 'em Out of Circulation: Does Incarceration of Juvenile Offenders Reduce Crime?" *Journal of Criminal Law and Criminology*, vol. 65, no. 4 (1974):528-535.

25. Jacqueline Cohen, "The Incapacitative Effect" 201-203.

26. James J. Collins, Jr., "Chronic Offender Careers," Presented at the Annual Meeting of the American Society of Criminology, Tucson, Arizona, 4-7 November 1976. See also Marvin E. Wolfgang, "From Boy to Man—From Delinquency to Crime," Presented at the National Symposium on the Serious Juvenile Offender, Minneapolis, Minnesota, 19-20 September 1977.

27. Marvin E. Wolfgang and James J. Collins, Jr., *Offender Careers and Restraint: Probabilities and Policy Implications* (Final Report to the National Institute of Juvenile Justice and Delinquency Prevention, 1977) 104.

28. Ibid., 124.

29. Jacqueline Cohen, "The Incapacitative Effect" 208-209.

3

Prevention Through Incapacitation

The Criminal Careers of the 342 Subjects of the Study

The central problem of this study is the effectiveness of a policy of incapacitating sentences in the reduction of violent crime. Difficulties immediately arose in devising a strategy for research. They have plagued us in the conceptualization, they aroused controversy in discussions with colleagues, and they can never be resolved to everyone's satisfaction. The reader will discover that we have made some arbitrary decisions, and we know that each such decision is open to the challenge that an alternate course might have led to a different result. But coherence is maintained by consistency and a resistance to unlimited exploration of complexity. What we have to report is intricate enough without digressing into the exploration of every possible speculation.

The first difficulty was the definition of the universe of violent crime. As every criminologist knows, the real total is impossible to obtain. Not even the most elaborate victimization survey can arrive at that certainty, but it is well established that far more crimes are committed than are reported to the police.[1] Although surveys have been conducted in many American cities, Columbus, Ohio has not been included. We had no choice but to use the figures compiled by the Federal Bureau of Investigation and published in the annual *Uniform Crime Reports.* Our geographical base was Franklin County, in which Columbus is located. Our base in time was the year 1973, but because many of the crimes for which indictments were made occurred in 1972, we divided the total for the two years to give us an average number for the violent crimes reported in the two years. For convenience, we shall talk of the offenses as 1973 crime. The firm total for the number of index violent crimes for the 28 reporting departments in Franklin County was 2,892, a number to which we will return again and frequently.

That number contains some internal discrepancies of which we must be aware, even though we can do little to offset them. In addition to its fractional representation of the full extent of violent crime, it conceals great variations in the reporting of different kinds of crime. We know from the victimization surveys in comparable cities that the number of violent crimes known to the police is less than 40 percent of those reported to surveyors.[2] What is at least as important to understand is that reporting rates range from less than 30 percent for some offenses to more than 70 percent for others. The pattern varies from city to city. In our neighboring metropolis of Cincinnati only 44 percent of all crimes against the person were reported. From crime to crime, however, the range was from 71 percent of robberies with serious injury to 27 percent for attempted robbery without injury.

Of these 2,892 serious personal injury crimes, 638 were cleared by the arrest of 342 adult offenders. An additional 154 offenses were cleared by the arrest of 126 juveniles. The latter figure may be low; police processing of juvenile offenders differs from the handling of adults, especially in recording procedures. Proceeding with caution, we arrive at a total of 792 offenses attributable to 468 persons arrested, of whom 73 percent were adults. About 90 percent of those arrested had addresses within Columbus.

We must now describe this unlucky assortment of violent offenders who were arrested, bearing in mind that in that respect they differ from an unknown number of luckier offenders who escaped apprehension. Our sources are the official data, collected for administrative purposes and without concern for the requirements of research. At least as to the broad demographic variables they leave little room for doubt as to validity. Anyone reviewing them must again be impressed by the evidence that it is the poor, the black, and the disadvantaged who are most frequently arrested for crimes. Whatever the implications for the administration of justice may be (and we are sure that they are disturbing to those who must manage the system), these findings emphasize the stubborn pathology of American culture, even in such a relatively healthy city as Columbus.

The 342 Arrestees

In this section we examine the criminal histories and personal characteristics of the 342 adults charged with violent felonies and whose cases were completed in the Franklin County Court of Common Pleas during the year 1973. The 342 are the total population, the universe, of persons booked for violent crimes during the interval. It should be noted that the criminal records discussed in the first portion of the chapter include the records of these subjects both as adults and as juveniles; we use the term *career record* when we wish to discuss the combined juvenile and adult record.

Sex. Only five of the 342 persons arrested were women. Except for murder, the violent crimes are almost exclusively reserved for men. Nearly seventy men were arrested for every one woman. If the findings of our study point to any policy, it certainly indicates no need at present for incapacitating sentences for women in the interest of reducing crime. (See table 3-1.)

Race. As usual in such studies, blacks were heavily overrepresented. The population in Columbus in 1970 was 18.5 percent black while the population of

Table 3-1
Race and Sex Distributions of 342 Persons Arrested for Violent Crimes

Race	Males		Females	
	Number	*Percent*	*Number*	*Percent*
Black	199	58.2	3	0.9
White	138	40.4	2	0.6

the county was only 12.6 percent black.[3] In our cohort, however, blacks outnumbered whites by about three to two. (See table 3-1.) Columbus also has a large population of Appalachian migrants, most of whom are poor. Were it not for this component of our cohort, for which we are unable to make a definite statistical estimate, the black-white ratio would have been substantially higher.

Age. As a group the cohort was young. Over 70 percent were under thirty; it is interesting to note that about 16 percent of the black males were above that age, as compared to 28 percent of the white males. As more blacks committed robbery, and as robbery is a youthful pursuit, this discrepancy seems readily understandable. (See table 3-2.)

Socioeconomic Status. Since the police do not regularly record the education and occupation of those arrested but do obtain residence addresses, the latter was used as an indicator of social class. We classified 306 addresses by census tract; the median income of each of the 306 tracts was determined. Thirty-six offenders with addresses that were not known or were from outside the county were not categorized. The cases were classified by the median income of the tract in which the individual resided as compared with the median income for all tracts in Franklin County. The median income for all tracts at the time of the study was $10,582.

Of our 342 violent offenders, thirty-eight (11.1 percent) lived in tracts in which the median income was less than half the county-wide median, or $5,291. Eighty-eight percent of the cases lived in tracts in which income was below the median; only forty-one subjects came from tracts with median incomes above the county-wide median. (See table 3-3.)

Career Felony Conviction History. Offenders who have never been convicted of felonies could not have been incapacitated. It is striking that over half of our subjects had no previous felony conviction, either adult or juvenile, when arrested in 1973. About 16 percent had one conviction; 12 percent had two; 18 percent had three or more. (See table 3-4.)

The distribution of prior felony convictions by race produces a difference of dubious significance. Of the 138 white males among our subjects, eighty-one

Table 3-2
Age, Race, and Sex of 342 Persons Arrested for Violent Crimes

Age	Black Male		White Male		Black Female		White Female		Total	
	Number	Percent	Number	Percent	Number	Percent	Number	Percent	Number	Percent
Under 21	56	(28.1)	35	(25.7)	2	(66.7)	0	(0.0)	93	(27.2)
21-25	73	(36.7)	47	(34.1)	0	(0.0)	1	(50.0)	121	(35.4)
26-30	39	(19.6)	17	(12.3)	0	(0.0)	0	(0.0)	56	(16.4)
31-40	20	(10.1)	19	(13.8)	0	(0.0)	1	(50.0)	40	(11.7)
41-50	5	(2.5)	10	(7.1)	1	(33.3)	0	(0.0)	16	(4.7)
51+	6	(3.1)	10	(7.1)	0	(0.0)	0	(0.0)	16	(4.7)
Total	199	(100.1)	138	(100.1)	3	(100.0)	2	(100.0)	342	(100.1)[a]

[a]Error due to rounding.

Table 3-3
Median Income in Tract of Residence of 342 Persons Arrested for Violent Crime

Income	Number	Percent
Below $5,291	38	11.1
$5,292-$8,465	135	39.5
$8,466-$10,582	92	26.9
Above $10,582	41	12.0
Not known	36	10.5
Total	342	100.0

(58.7 percent) had prior felony convictions, but ninety-six of the 199 black males (48.2 percent) were without prior convictions. We do not regard this difference as of any practical importance, nor do we consider the slightly higher percentage of blacks than whites who were chronic (five or more convictions) of any heuristic value. (See table 3-5.)

The lack of any significant relationship between age and the absence of a prior conviction may in itself be significant. It is to be expected that some young offenders will bring a clean slate to court; every criminal career has to begin at some point and most careers start early. In our cohort, fifty-four of the ninety-three subjects under twenty-one had no prior career conviction; of the 217 subjects in the twenty-one to forty age range just under half were free of a record of prior convictions. But in the oldest range, forty-one and over, five-eighths of the cases were without prior career convictions. There were only thirty-two in this last category, but the proportion of clear records reminds us that older offenders are not necessarily chronic offenders. Where the crime is violent, the occasion may have been the sudden destruction of a fabric of living rather than the continuing accretion of a lifetime of criminal incidents.

Table 3-4
Prior Career Felony Convictions of 342 Subjects

Prior Felony Convictions	Number	Percent
0	181	52.9
1	56	16.4
2	42	12.3
3	22	6.4
4	20	5.8
5	8	2.3
6	8	2.3
7	3	0.9
8	2	0.6
Total	342	99.9[a]

[a]Error due to rounding.

Table 3-5
Number of Prior Career Felony Convictions by Race and Sex

| | | | | | | | Number of Prior Career Felony Convictions | | | | | | | | |
| | 0 | | 1 | | 2 | | 3 | | 4 | | 5 or more | |
Race and Sex	Number	Percent	Number	Percent	Number	Percent	Number	Percent	Number	Percent	Number	Percent
Black males	96	48.2	34	17.1	26	13.1	15	7.5	13	6.5	15	7.5
White males	81	58.7	21	15.2	16	11.6	7	5.1	7	5.1	6	4.3
Black females	2	66.7	1	33.3	—	—	—	—	—	—	—	—
White females	2	100.0	—	—	—	—	—	—	—	—	—	—

Table 3-6
Prior Career-Violent Convictions of 342 Persons Arrested
for Violent Crimes

Prior Career-Violent Convictions	Number	Percent
0	280	81.9
1	46	13.5
2	10	2.9
3	6	1.8
Total	342	100.1[a]

[a]Error due to rounding.

Career-Violent Felony Convictions. Of these 337 putatively violent male offenders, 275 had never before been convicted of a violent crime, either as a juvenile or adult; 46 had one such conviction, ten had two, and six had three—none had more than three. (See table 3-6.) None of the five female offenders had any prior convictions of a violent crime. Eighty-seven percent of the white males were without priors, as compared to 77.9 percent of the blacks—a difference sufficient to notice but hardly of significance for planners and decision-makers. (See table 3-7.) It is possible, of course, that some of that difference may be accounted for by plea bargaining, but our records do not provide particulars about the degree to which negotiations of this kind affected dispositions.

Regardless of age, our subjects were without prior violent felony convictions in four out of five cases. The variation from age group to age group was slight, as will be seen in table 3-8. We noted that three of the sixteen subjects in the over fifty age group had three convictions apiece—the remaining thirteen of their peers had none. Violent losers of this degree of chronicity probably should be subjected to extended incapacitation, if a policy could be devised to hold them

Table 3-7
Prior Career-Violent Convictions by Race and Sex of 342 Persons
Arrested for Violent Crime

Race and Sex	Number and Percent of Prior Violent Convictions				
	0	1	2	3	Total
Black male	155 (77.9)	33 (16.6)	8 (4.0)	3 (1.5)	199
White male	120 (87.0)	13 (9.4)	2 (1.4)	3 (2.2)	138
Black female	3 (100.0)	0 (0.0)	0 (0.0)	0 (0.0)	3
White female	2 (100.0)	0 (0.0)	0 (0.0)	0 (0.0)	2
Total	280 (81.9)	46 (13.5)	10 (2.9)	6 (1.8)	342

Table 3-8
Prior Career-Violent Convictions by Age of 342 Persons
Arrested for Violent Crime

	Number and Percentage of Prior Career-Violent Convictions				
	0	1	2	3	Total
Under 21	79 (84.9)	10 (10.8)	3 (3.2)	1 (1.1)	93
21-25	97 (80.1)	21 (17.4)	3 (2.5)	0 (0.0)	121
26-30	44 (78.5)	10 (17.9)	1 (1.8)	1 (1.8)	56
31-40	32 (80.0)	4 (10.0)	3 (7.5)	1 (2.5)	40
41-50	15 (93.8)	1 (6.3)	0 (0.0)	0 (0.0)	16
51+	13 (81.3)	0 (0.0)	0 (0.0)	3 (18.8)	16
Total	280 (81.9)	46 (13.5)	10 (2.9)	6 (1.8)	342

without at the same time holding individuals whose criminal careers have come to an end. The extreme length of the criminal careers of the three further complicates the issue. The first offenses of the three occurred twenty-eight, thirty, and forty years before the 1973 arrests. The dimensions of the problem are small: The three senior triple losers were half of the recidivists of their class in the entire cohort. We note also that there were only ten men with two prior violent felony convictions around whose cases a policy of augmented restraint could be designed.

Crimes and Prosecutions

All of the 342 adult offenders in our cohort were arrested for violent offenses, thereby qualifying them as violent offenders, the only ones officially recognized as such in the year 1973. But they were not specialists in violence. Most of their prior arrests were for property offenses. In all, they had been charged over their adult and juvenile careers with 798 felony offenses, an average of 2.3. It will be seen from table 3-9 that burglary, auto theft, and larceny constitute about half the offenses charged. There were three murder charges, forty-eight armed robberies, fourteen rapes, sixty-five unarmed robberies, forty aggravated assaults, and a handful of other offenses in which shooting, stabbing, or other violence was an element.

Scrutiny of table 3-9 also brings out a consistency in the criminal careers of our subjects. At whatever stage of a career an offense may occur, it is most likely to be an index property offense. First offenses are predominately burglary, auto theft, and larceny—so are third and sixth offenses. Experience does not seem to lead the veteran criminal into any specialties discernible in a statistical distribution like this.

Table 3-10 displays a relatively constant desistance rate through the first eight offenses, after which the number of cases diminishes to a point of insignificance for analysis. Of the first-time arrestees, fifty-six, or 26.5 percent were arrested for no more offenses. Thirty-nine of the second offenders (25.2 percent) desisted. If arrest activity is representative of real criminal activity, then the pattern suggests that most of our subjects, once embarked on a second offense, will continue on to a third, fourth or fifth offense. Violent offenses are sprinkled randomly through their careers with no indication that they necessarily occur early or late.

Table 3-11 brings out an oddity for which we have no certain explanation. Of the 211 subjects charged with a first felony, 61.1 percent were found guilty as charged on that felony. Of the 155 with a second felony charge, 57.4 percent were guilty as charged. The comparable percentages, it will be noted, decline to 33.3 percent for those with a sixth felony charge. The same trend, with a less regular curve, was displayed when we added subjects charged with felonies but convicted of misdemeanors. We must suppose that some of our subjects had learned a trick or two from long experience in criminal justice so that charges which might have been sustained were dismissed. Police harassment may have occurred; sometimes an offender might be arrested on charges that could not be accepted by the prosecutor. Whatever the explanation, it is true for this cohort that the longer the career the less likely the individual is to be found guilty as charged on the nth offenses.

Offenses, Findings, and Dispositions

We come now to an account of what our subjects did and what was done with them by the prosecutor and the courts. Table 3-12 displays the entire range of the charges against them—from first degree murder to various attempts to commit crimes of violence. In all, there were 638 charges of personal injury crimes against our subjects, an average of 1.9 charges per cohort member.

For the purposes of our study, a crucial finding is that a search of the Columbus juvenile files and FBI arrest records showed that 181 of these 342 individuals had no prior adult or juvenile felony conviction of any kind, and thus could not have been incapacitated for the 1973 offense charged against them. Many of these individuals must have committed their offenses as impulsive responses to the situation confronting them, sometimes under the distortions of alcohol or drug, sometimes by a transitory loss of control in a condition of fear or anger. No incapacitation policy is going to prevent many crimes committed under these circumstances. It is likely that our cohort is fairly representative of experience elsewhere, and that a large number of the violent crimes cleared by the police are of this character—first offenses committed under stresses and influences inaccessible to the preventive processes of the law.

Table 3-9

Distribution of Arrests by Type of Crime and Offense Sequence Number

Offense Type	Offense Sequence Number												Total Arrests
	1	2	3	4	5	6	7	8	9	10	11	12	
Murder I	2	—	1	—	—	—	—	—	—	—	—	—	3
Armed robbery	12	10	9	7	6	2	1	1	—	—	—	—	48
Rape	3	2	3	2	1	2	1	—	—	—	—	—	14
Unarmed robbery	13	13	9	10	6	7	5	1	1	—	—	—	65
Carnal knowledge of female under 16	2	—	—	—	1	—	—	—	—	—	—	—	3
Manslaughter I	1	1	—	1	—	—	—	—	—	—	—	—	3
Intentional shooting	2	—	—	—	1	—	—	—	—	—	—	—	3
Sodomy	—	1	—	—	—	—	—	—	—	—	—	—	1
Assault to kill	2	—	—	—	—	—	—	1	—	1	—	—	4
Assault to rape	2	—	—	—	1	—	—	—	—	1	—	—	4
Assault to rob	—	—	1	—	1	—	—	1	1	—	—	—	4
Assault on minor	2	2	1	—	—	—	1	—	1	—	—	—	7
Aggravated assault	8	8	11	4	4	3	1	—	1	—	—	—	40
Inducing illicit intercourse	—	—	—	1	—	—	—	—	—	—	—	—	1
Burglary	42	27	18	15	11	6	6	4	2	—	—	—	131
Breaking and entering	22	12	13	5	8	7	1	4	2	—	—	—	74
Malicious entry	—	1	1	—	—	—	—	1	1	—	—	—	4
Burglary from auto	—	3	—	—	—	—	—	1	1	—	—	—	5
Breaking and entering at night	—	—	1	—	—	—	—	—	—	—	—	—	1
Forced entry	1	—	—	—	—	—	—	—	—	—	—	—	1
Prowling	1	—	—	—	—	—	—	—	—	—	—	—	1
Receiving and concealing	2	1	1	3	1	2	1	2	—	—	—	—	13
Breaking and entering safety deposits	2	—	—	—	2	—	—	—	—	—	—	—	4
Possession of criminal tools	1	1	1	—	—	1	—	—	—	—	—	—	4
Burglary of auto	—	1	—	—	—	—	—	—	—	—	—	—	1
Auto theft	41	33	17	12	8	6	1	4	3	3	—	—	128
Operating motor vehicle without owner's consent	5	4	2	4	2	—	2	—	—	—	—	—	19
Dyer Act	2	—	—	—	—	—	—	—	—	—	—	—	2
Carrying concealed weapon	—	—	2	1	2	—	1	1	—	—	1	—	8

Offense												Total
Possession of firearm by felon	—	—	—	—	—	—	—	—	—	—	—	1	1
Larceny	29	15	12	13	11	5	7	3	4	3	1	1	104
Larceny from dwelling	—	—	—	1	1	1	—	—	—	—	—	—	1
Mail theft	—	1	—	—	1	—	1	—	—	—	—	—	3
Theft of interstate shipment	—	—	—	—	—	—	1	—	—	—	1	—	2
Larceny by trick	6	6	6	4	3	4	—	—	2	3	1	—	1
Forgery	—	1	—	—	—	1	—	1	1	—	1	—	37
Forgery of sales slips	1	—	—	—	—	—	—	—	—	—	—	—	3
Defraud innkeeper	1	1	1	—	—	—	—	—	—	—	—	—	1
Executing and delivering insufficient funds	—	—	—	—	—	—	—	—	—	1	—	—	2
Uttering and publishing forged checks	—	1	1	—	—	—	—	—	—	—	1	—	2
Fraud	—	—	1	1	1	1	—	2	—	1	—	—	1
Possession of narcotics	4	6	4	6	1	1	—	—	—	—	—	—	25
Possession of narcotics for sale	1	2	1	1	—	1	—	—	—	—	—	—	5
Possession of drug instruments	—	2	—	1	1	—	—	—	—	—	—	—	1
Arson	1	—	—	—	—	1	—	—	—	—	—	—	4
Embezzlement of government property	1	—	1	—	—	—	—	—	—	—	—	—	1
Malicious destruction	—	—	—	—	—	—	—	—	—	—	—	—	1
Attempt to burn property	—	—	—	—	1	—	—	—	—	—	—	—	1
Attempted abortion	—	1	—	1	1	—	—	—	—	—	—	—	1
White slave act	—	—	—	1	—	—	—	—	—	—	—	—	2
Incest	—	—	—	1	—	—	—	—	—	—	—	—	1
Perjury	—	—	—	—	—	—	1	—	—	—	—	—	1
Embezzlement	—	—	—	—	—	—	—	—	—	—	—	—	1
Total	211	155	116	95	74	51	35	25	18	12	4	2	798

Table 3-10
Rate of Career Persistence in Felony Activity

Number of Prior Felony Arrests	Number of Cases	Rate of Persistence	Number of Desistors
1	211	—	
2	155	73.5	56
3	116	74.8	39
4	95	81.9	21
5	74	77.9	21
6	51	68.9	23
7	35	68.6	16
8	25	71.4	10
9	18	72.0	7
10	12	66.7	6
11	4	33.3	8
12	2	50.0	2

Dispositions by Prosecutor and Court

Once the police have arrested a suspect, the next decision must be made by the county prosecutor. First he has to decide whether he is to proceed with litigation, a decision that depends on the quality of the evidence and the willingness of the witnesses to testify. If in his judgment these elements are critically lacking, he may enter a motion of *nolle prosequi* in municipal court. However, this does not seem to have occurred in Franklin County in 1973.

For those felony cases which are arraigned and on which the county

Table 3-11
Percentage of Subjects Found Guilty of Felony or Misdemeanor by Felony Offense Number

Number of Prior Felony Arrest	Number of Cases	Percent Guilty of a Felony	Percent Guilty of Felony or Misdemeanor
1	211	61.1	71.6
2	155	57.4	65.2
3	116	50.9	60.3
4	95	48.2	58.9
5	74	41.9	62.2
6	51	33.3	49.0
7	35	42.9	54.2
8	25	48.0	56.0
9	18	27.7	55.6
10	12	50.0	58.3
11	4	50.0	50.0
12	2	0.0	50.0

Table 3-12
Distribution of Instant Offense of 342 Subjects

Category	Number	Percent
Murder I	34	9.9
Murder II	9	2.6
Armed robbery	101	29.5
Rape female under 14	1	0.3
Maiming	2	0.6
Rape	30	8.8
Unarmed robbery	52	15.2
Carnal knowledge of female under 16[a]	18	5.3
Manslaughter I	6	1.8
Intentional shooting	15	4.4
Sodomy[a]	13	3.8
Attempted rape female under 14	2	0.6
Assault to kill	4	1.2
Assault to rape	7	2.0
Assault to rob	8	2.3
Assault on minor	9	2.6
Aggravated assault	31	9.1
Total	342	100.0

[a]An examination of these cases indicated them to be violent.

prosecutor wishes to proceed, a presentation to the grand jury is made. In principle the grand jury makes its independent judgment as to whether the evidence justifies indictment. It may "no-bill" a charge despite the county prosecutor's wish to proceed. In all, fifty-three of the study group of 342 were "no-billed."

After the indictment by the grand jury, the county prosecutor may still drop a case in which he thinks there is little chance of conviction (or in exchange for a plea of guilty on another charge). At this point the motion of *nolle prosequi* can again be made, this time in the court of common pleas. In principle, the court may deny the motion, but so far as we have been able to learn, this happens rarely, if ever, in Franklin County. Forty-four of the study group were pronounced innocent in this way. Four more cases were dismissed for reasons having to do with mental status; they found their way to the Lima State Hospital for the criminally insane. Finally, of the 241 who finally reached the court of common pleas for disposition, twenty-six were found not guilty. That left 215 subjects who either pled guilty or were found guilty after trial of the original charge or of a lesser offense as agreed in plea bargaining. Table 3-13 shows one additional case in which final disposition is uncertain, apparently a situation in which the defendant was committed to a state hospital as a mentally ill offender.

It will be shown later that only 166 of our 342 subjects (48.5 percent) were

Table 3-13
Prosecutorial and Judicial Decisions in Instant Offense

Category	Number	Percent
No bill	52	12.9
Nolle Prosequi	44	15.2
Dismissed by magistrate	4	1.2
Not guilty	26	7.6
Guilty	215	62.9
Other	1	0.3
Total	342	100.0

found guilty of a violent offense. They were guilty on 231 charges, 8 percent of the 2,892 violent crimes reported to the police in 1973 and 36 percent of the 638 crimes charged against our cohort. Whatever goal of criminal justice is given primacy, the efficiency of the system thus falls into serious question. A system which can clear through arrest only a small fraction of the crimes reported, and secure convictions for only a minority of the crimes for which arrests were made can hardly be said to achieve the goal of predictability; the public must conclude that the chances are good of escaping justice even after the commission of a serious crime. Certainly the ends of retribution and deterrence are not being met, and incapacitation takes place only with respect to specific individuals who might commit future crimes. It is not to be expected that the rates of violent crime can be significantly reduced by the imprisonment of the 128 individuals who received sentences to long-term incarceration. (See table 3-14.)

Table 3-14
Sanction Imposed in Instant Offense

Category	Number	Percent
Not guilty	122	35.7
Penalty suspended	5	1.5
Fine or restitution	9	2.6
Jail	10	2.9
Jail and fine or restitution	1	0.3
Jail and probation	4	1.2
Probation plus fine or restitution	13	3.8
Probation	42	12.3
Prison plus shock probation	16	4.7
Reformatory	60	17.5
Prison	52	15.2
Lima State Hospital	8	2.3
Total	342	100.0

We do not consider that a legitimate claim of injustice can be made with respect to any individual found guilty of a specific crime and sentenced according to the law. But human nature being what it is, the offenders who were unlucky enough to receive the full brunt of the law may at least be understood if they sense an unfairness in a system which caught and punished them while others, no doubt just as guilty or more so, go free. This sense of unfairness must be enhanced by the observation that those who are in the same plight are poor, young, and black. In the abstractions of the higher jurisprudence no cognizance can be taken of this sense of inequity; it is enough that those who are caught and found guilty should suffer the penalty of the law. But this symbolic retribution at best conveys a fear of the law without instilling respect. That the fear is so uncertain, so much of an invitation to gamble, must limit its usefulness in the control of crime.

Predicting Decisions

Using multidiscriminant function analysis, we attempted to assess the predictability of the system in which our 342 subjects were enmeshed. Three kinds of variables were combined to create a system which successfully predicted the guilt of those found guilty in 98.6 percent of the cases. The variables consisted of first, the available demographic factors, (age, race, sex, and socioeconomic status); second, the crimes charged, (homicide, rape, assault, and robbery); and third, the criminal history variables, (number of prior arrests, number of prior convictions, previous prison sentences, and the number of previous violent felony convictions).

The system worked well in predicting adjudications of guilt, but only by predicting that almost every one would be guilty. Nothing else could be predicted at an acceptable level of accuracy. Table 3-15 shows the results of our attempt to forecast the outcome of the prosecutor's case management. The system correctly predicted 98.6 percent of the findings of guilt. It incorrectly predicted that 93.2 percent of those who were actually given a declaration of *nolle prosequi* would be found guilty and that all those whom the grand jury refused to indict would be found guilty.

Table 3-16 limits the outcome to a distinction between guilt and innocence. The results are scarcely better. We designated all cases found not guilty, no-billed or, given a writ of *nolle prosequi*, as not guilty, and partitioned the various degrees of guilt into four classes: guilty of a misdemeanor, guilty of a nonviolent felony, guilty of a violent felony, and guilty but insane. The effectiveness of prediction scarcely exceeded chance. Proceeding on a diagonal from the upper left to the lower right of table 3-16, we find that the discriminant function analysis correctly predicts 35.5 percent of the 121 who were not guilty. Three of the twenty-eight found guilty of a misdemeanor were identified, but not one of

Table 3-15
Predicted and Actual Outcome at the Prosecutorial Level

Outcome	Total Cases	Predicted Outcome (Number and Percent)			
		No Bill	Nolle Prosequi	Not Found Guilty	Guilty
No bill	52	0	0	0	52
	100	0.0%	0.0%	0.0%	100.0%
Nolle Prosequi	44	0	3	0	41
	100	0.0%	6.8%	0.0%	93.2%
Not found guilty	31	0	0	1	30
	100	0.0%	0.0%	3.2%	96.8%
Guilty	215	0	2	1	212
	100	0.0%	0.9%	0.5%	98.6%

Note: Percent of "grouped" cases correctly classified is 63.16.

the eighteen subjects who were found guilty of a nonviolent felony—by plea bargaining in most cases—was picked up. But of the 169 (including a few insanity cases) who were found guilty of a violent felony, 134 (79.3 percent) were predicted. In the former, all findings of guilt at any level are aggregated in one sum; in the latter, we are attempting to predict different levels of guilt with indifferent success.

As to predicting sentences, the capability of the system disintegrated as shown in table 3-17. Probation was correctly predicted in two out of fifty-five cases; "shock" probation (which, in Ohio, provides for a brief prison internment) was predicted in one out of sixteen cases. The system was more effective in predicting prison and reformatory sentences: 30 percent in the case of reformatory commitments, 36.5 percent in the case of prison.

This analysis indicates the powerful influence of subjective factors in criminal justice decision-making. It might be supposed that criminal histories and the nature of the instant offense would constitute the primary determinant in sentencing. That is far from the case. Criminal justice is a system that processes people and must be dependent on the judgments of the people who administer it. This subjectivity is no doubt inevitable, but the degree to which discretion reduces predictability has an impact on the usefulness of the criminal justice system in the control of crime. These results also indicate the problems inherent in the use of multidiscriminant function analysis in dealing with complex outcomes dependent on subjective variables such as determinations of insanity and competence and on plea bargaining. These predictive inadequacies tend to limit the applicability of finely tuned mathematical and statistical procedures to qualitative and variable data.

The Effectiveness of Incapacitation on Adult Crime Only

The remainder of this chapter will be devoted to a consideration of the effectiveness of various incapacitating sentencing strategies. This problem should

Table 3-16
Predicted and Actual Findings of Guilt

Outcome	Total Cases	Predicted Outcome (Number and Percent)				
		Not Guilty	Guilty-Misdemeanor	Guilty-Nonviolent Felony	Guilty-Violent Felony	Insanity
Not guilty	121	43	0	0	74	4
	100	35.5%	0.0%	0.0%	61.2%	3.3%
Guilty-misdemeanor	28	11	3	0	14	0
	100	39.3%	10.7%	0.0%	50.0%	0.0%
Guilty-nonviolent felony	18	6	2	0	10	0
	100	33.3%	11.1%	0.0%	55.6%	0.0%
Guilty-violent felony	169	28	1	1	134	5
	100	16.6%	0.6%	0.6%	79.3%	3.0%
Insanity	6	2	0	0	0	4
	100	33.3%	0.0%	0.0%	0.0%	66.7%

Note: Percent of "grouped" cases correctly classified is 53.80.

Table 3-17
Predicted and Actual Penalties Assessed

Penalty	Total Cases	Predicted Penalty (Number and Percent)						
		Not Guilty	Some Penalty	Probation	Prison Plus Shock	Reformatory	Prison	Lima State/ Psychiatric Facility
Not guilty	122 100	97 79.5%	0 0.0%	2 1.6%	1 0.8%	6 4.9%	13 10.7%	3 2.5%
Some penalty[a]	29 100	21 72.4%	1 3.4%	0 0.0%	0 0.0%	2 6.9%	4 13.8%	1 3.4%
Probation	55 100	48 87.3%	1 1.8%	2 3.6%	0 0.0%	3 5.5%	0 0.0%	1 1.8%
Prison plus shock	16 100	13 81.3%	0 0.0%	0 0.0%	1 6.3%	1 6.3%	1 6.3%	0 0.0%
Reformatory	60 100	40 66.7%	0 0.0%	0 0.0%	0 0.0%	18 30.0%	2 3.3%	0 0.0%
Prison	52 100	29 55.8%	0 0.0%	0 0.0%	0 0.0%	3 5.8%	19 36.5%	1 1.9%
Lima State Hospital or psychiatric facility	8 100	5 62.5%	0 0.0%	0 0.0%	0 0.0%	0 0.0%	1 12.5%	2 25.0%

Note: Percent of "grouped" cases correctly classified is 40.94.
[a]Penalties include suspended sentence, fine, jail and restitution.

be viewed from three perspectives: from the point of view of preventing convicted (or even arrested) felons from committing subsequent violent crimes for a specified time period; of preventing as large a portion as possible of the violent crimes cleared in any year by incapacitating the most likely perpetrators on the basis of their prior criminal histories; by preventing a portion of the violent crimes at the conviction level. These questions reduce to two issues: (1) How much violent crime is likely to be prevented by a policy of sentencing for incapacitation? (2) How long must sentences be if incapacitation is to have a significant impact on the violent crime rate?

Breaking these questions down to produce answers relevant to policy, we tried to design a study which would illuminate the specific issues confronting the legislature in establishing sentencing limits and the courts in establishing actual terms of incarceration for offenders to be sentenced. We need to know the effectiveness of various incapacitation policies in reducing the incidence of homicide, robbery, aggravated assault, and forcible rape. How many of these crimes would be prevented by the incarceration of repetitively violent criminals for periods of three or five years? Of violators with previous histories of nonviolent offenses only? Of those under some specific age level reserved for the juvenile court? Of those with prior juvenile court contact? In short, what can the criminal histories of actual offenders tell us about the optimal sentencing policies if the reduction of violent crime is to be the object of an incapacitation strategy? In a recent publication, we discussed the manner in which we addressed these and related questions.

We collected all recorded data on every person charged with each of the violent crimes enumerated above in Franklin County (Columbus), Ohio in 1973.[4] In 1973, 364 adults were arrested and charged with one or more murders and manslaughters, robberies, aggravated assaults, and violent sex offenses. Of these 364 persons, fourteen were charged with violent crimes committed while in prison or as escapees from a penal institution. These fourteen cases were eliminated from the universe of eligible subjects. Also excluded were eight subjects for whom no previous criminal histories could be found in the files of the Columbus Police Department, the Franklin County Sheriff's Department, the Ohio Bureau of Criminal Identification, the FBI, or the Ohio Department of Rehabilitation and Corrections. Elimination of the fourteen prison inmates and escapees and the eight persons with missing files reduced the cohort to 342 subjects.

The 342 remaining individuals met the following criteria. All were adults or juveniles bound over and charged as adults. All had been indicted or arraigned for one of the major personal crimes [listed in table 3-12]. All were listed by the Franklin County Prosecutor as "disposed of" (cases completed) during the 1973 calendar year. The Prosecutor "disposes of" a person charged with a crime in one of four ways: the grand jury decides not to indict; a plea of *nolle prosequi* is entered by the prosecutor; the case proceeds to trial and the defendant is acquitted; or the defendant pleads guilty or is so found in the trial. A case is not considered complete until the immediate appeals are concluded.[5]

Of our cohort of 342 Franklin County violent offenders in 1973, 166 were found guilty as charged. The remainder, 176 cases, were distributed between the two-thirds who were released on writs of *nolle prosequi* and no-bills, and the other third, who, after plea bargaining, pled guilty to a lesser offense or were declared insane. The cohort was divided accordingly into two groups, those who were found guilty as charged, and those who were charged but not convicted on the violent crime charge. Our analysis separates these two groups throughout.

Nevertheless it is essential to understand that our basic assumption holds that *all subjects in the cohort, whether found guilty or not of the crimes with which they were charged, did in fact commit all the crimes for which they were arrested.* Thus a man who was arrested for fourteen robberies but tried and convicted on only three, is assumed, for the purpose of this study, to have comitted all fourteen. If he had been subjected to a mandatory sentence on his last previous conviction of a felony, the resulting incapacitation would be counted as preventing all fourteen offenses. This assumption deliberately overstates the effectiveness of an incapacitation policy. We are interested here in exploring the maximum potential of imprisonment in the prevention of crime; this assumption yields a maximum estimate of the official effectiveness of adult incapacitation policies, as far as our data will let us go. To develop a minimum estimate of effectiveness, we compare convictions prevented to the number of crimes committed.

The uses of official records have serious limitations well known to criminologists. It would have been desirable to complete our analysis by presenting the influence of the variables of socioeconomic status, educational level, employment histories and other items of social differentiation, but the only uniform social information available identified those under study by age, race, sex, and place of residence.

To test the effectiveness of incapacitation, we needed to determine how many of the 1973 offenses would have been prevented if an incapacitating sentence had been imposed at the last previous conviction.

Sentencing Policies

There were eighteen theoretical sentencing policies to be considered based on three criteria: number of prior felony convictions, whether violent or nonviolent, and length of incapacitating sentence. Arrayed in tabular form, the eighteen sentencing policies are as follows. (See table 3-18.)

It is obvious that Policies 13 and 16 are impossible options. There can be no

Table 3-18
Sentencing Policies Based on Prior Felonies, Prior Violent
Felonies, and Length of Sentence

Sentencing Policy	Number of Prior Felony Convictions	Number of Prior Violent Felony Convictions	Years of Incapacitation
1	1	0	3
2	2	0	3
3	3	0	3
4	1	0	5
5	2	0	5
6	3	0	5
7	1	1	3
8	2	1	3
9	3	1	3
10	1	1	5
11	2	1	5
12	3	1	5
13[a]	1	2	3
14	2	2	3
15	3	2	3
16[a]	1	2	5
17	2	2	5
18	3	2	5

[a]Policy is clearly impossible.

greater number of convictions for violent felonies than for all felonies combined. All of these policies will be presented. Special attention, however, will be devoted to the five most important alternatives including Policy 4, the most stringent option. These five hypothetical sentencing policies are, as follows:

Sentencing Policy 1: Assume that on any felony conviction, whether violent or not, a three-year net mandatory prison term was imposed.

Sentencing Policy 4: Assume that on any felony conviction, whether violent or not, a five-year net mandatory prison term was imposed.

Sentencing Policy 5: Assume that on any felony conviction after the first (second and following), whether violent or not, a five-year net mandatory prison term was imposed. On the first conviction the penalty structure continues as under present law.

Sentencing Policy 6: Assume that on any felony conviction after the second (third and following), whether violent or not, a five-year net mandatory prison term was imposed. On the first two convictions the penalty structure continues as under the present law.

Sentencing Policy 10: Assume that on any first violent felony conviction, a five-year net mandatory prison term was imposed. For any subsequent violent or nonviolent felony by the same offender, a five-year net mandatory prison term was imposed. For offenders convicted of only nonviolent felonies, the penalty structure continues as under the present law.

All policies apply and were imposed at the last previous conviction, that is, between 1968 and 1973. If that had been done how many of the 1973 crimes could not have occurred?

The adult histories of the 342 convicted 1973 violent offenders were examined to obtain the following information:

1. Did they have any previous adult felony conviction?
2. Were any such convictions for prior violent crimes as adults?
3. When was the last adult felony conviction recorded prior to the 1973 conviction?
4. Would the imposition of a three- or five-year net sentence for the earlier violation have prevented the 1973 offense? Would any of the 342 have been in prison under a stiffer earlier sentence and consequently been incapable of the 1973 murder/manslaughter, robbery, aggravated assault, or violent sex offense?

Each case in the cohort was reviewed to provide an answer to each of these questions. In addition to arrest and court records, the FBI arrest histories were also examined and coded. In this way each case in the sample could be evaluated to determine the effect of a mandatory sentence of the length called for in each option for each offender meeting the criteria of the options under evaluation.

A detailed review of the race, sex, age, socioeconomic status, career criminal histories (including juvenile and adult), the instant (1973) offense(s) charged, and the case outcomes have already been presented. (See tables 3-1, 3-2, 3-3 and 3-4.) We need only detail the adult criminal histories at this point. As adults, the criminal activities resulting in convictions can be described as follows: 67.8 percent had not been convicted of any felony offense while only 5.3 percent had three or more recorded convictions; 306 of the 342 had no prior convictions for any violent crime. As for the total career, neither race nor age was important in the adult history. (See tables 3-19, 3-20, 3-21, and 3-22.)

Findings

In our earlier mentioned paper, "The Incapacitation of the Previous Offender," we discuss our findings.[5] "Table 3-23 contains a distribution of the offenses for which they were indicted, the number of crimes with which they were charged, and the number of crimes charged per defendant. Robbery is by far the most

Table 3-19
**Prior Adult Felony Convictions of 342 Persons Arrested
for Violent Crimes**

Number of Prior Felony Convictions	Number	Percent
0	232	67.8
1	65	19.0
2	27	7.9
3	10	2.9
4	4	1.2
5	3	0.9
6	1	0.3
Total	342	100.0

frequent crime, and although this offense may be brutally violent, it may also be without violence inflicted or intended. Note also that if the robberies included under the separate heading of multiple offense category are combined with the robbery category, the total number of robbers would be 168, nearly half our universe. By the nature of this multiple offense category group, the robbers included in it must be presumed to be especially dangerous.

Attrition of the indictment sample is evident in table 3-24, which shows that only 166, or 48 percent, of the 342 persons indicted were convicted on violent charges for which they were indicted. Plea bargaining played an important role. Most of those convicted of a violent offense were convicted of fewer counts than the number for which they were indicted. Reduction of charges were quantitative as well as qualitative; it was not uncommon to find that eleven of fourteen robbery counts, for example, were dismissed, leaving three counts for the actual conviction. A robbery and rape in the indictment resulted in a rape conviction. As previously indicated, where charges were

Table 3-20
**Prior Adult Violent Convictions of 342 Persons Arrested for
Violent Crimes**

Prior Violent Convictions	Number	Percent
0	306	89.5
1	30	8.8
2	2	0.6
3	4	1.2
Total	342	100.1[a]

[a]Error due to rounding.

Table 3-21
Number of Prior Adult Felony Convictions by Race and Sex

| | | | | | | Number of Prior Felony Convictions | | | | | |
| | 0 | | 1 | | 2 | | 3 | | 4 | | 5 or more | |
Race and Sex	Number	Percent	Number	Percent	Number	Percent	Number	Percent	Number	Percent	Number	Percent
Black males	131	65.8	42	21.1	18	9.0	6	3.0	1	0.5	1	0.5
White males	96	69.6	23	16.7	9	6.5	4	2.9	3	2.2	3	2.1
Black females	3	100.0	—	—	—	—	—	—	—	—	—	—
White females	2	100.0	—	—	—	—	—	—	—	—	—	—

Table 3-22
**Prior Adult Violent Convictions by Age of 342 Persons Arrested
for Violent Crime**

Age	Number and Percentage of Prior Violent Felony Convictions				Total
	0	1	2	3	
18-21	91 (97.8)	2 (2.2)	0 (0.0)	0 (0.0)	93
21-25	109 (90.1)	12 (9.9)	0 (0.0)	0 (0.0)	121
26-30	46 (82.1)	10 (17.9)	0 (0.0)	0 (0.0)	56
31-40	32 (80.0)	5 (12.5)	2 (5.0)	1 (2.5)	40
41-50	15 (93.8)	1 (6.3)	0 (0.0)	0 (0.0)	16
51+	13 (81.3)	0 (0.0)	0 (0.0)	3 (18.8)	16
Total	306 (89.5)	30 (8.8)	2 (0.6)	4 (1.2)	342

dismissed in this manner, we counted them as actual offenses which might have been prevented by a policy of incapacitation.

As indicated in table 3-25, the 342 original members of the cohort were responsible for 638 offenses, which were cleared by their arrest. The 166 men who were convicted cleared only 231 offenses. These figures compare with the 2,892 violent index offenses reported in Franklin County in the 1973 *Uniform Crime Reports*. At the arrest level, the 638 charges represent 22.1 percent clearance on the reported violent crimes, but at the conviction level only 8.0

Table 3-23
**Distribution of Cohort by Crime of Indictment, Numbers of Crimes,
and Number of Crimes per Indictee**

	Persons Indicted	Crimes Charged, by Categories of Persons Indicted	Charges per Person
Murder/manslaughter	36	45	1.2
Robbery	128	269	2.1
Sex offenses (violent)	79	111	1.4
Assault	49	66	1.3
Multiple offense (two of the above)	50[a]	147[b]	2.9
Total	342	638	1.9

Source: Stephan Van Dine, Simon Dinitz, and John P. Conrad, "The Incapacitation of the Dangerous Offender: A Statistical Experiment," *Journal of Research in Crime and Delinquency*, vol. 14, no. 1 (1977):27. Reprinted with permission.

[a]Of the fifty persons, twenty-two were charged with robbery-assault offenses, twelve with robbery-sex offenses, six with murder/manslaughter-robbery offenses, six with murder/manslaughter-assault offenses, three with assault-sex offenses, and one with murder/manslaughter-sex offenses.

[b]The fifty persons charged with multiple offenses generated one hundred forty-seven charges, of which there were seventeen murder charges, fifty-five robbery charges, thirty-two sex offenses, and forty-three assault offenses.

Table 3-24

**Distribution of Cohort by Crime of Conviction, Number of
Convictions, and Number of Conviction-Counts per Offender**

	Persons Convicted	Conviction-Counts	Conviction-Counts per Offender
Murder/manslaughter	18	20	1.1
Robbery	77	100	1.3
Sex offenses (violent)	23	24	1.0
Assault	28	30	1.1
Multiple offense (two of the above)	20[a]	57[b]	2.8
Total	166	231	1.4

Source: Stephan Van Dine, Simon Dinitz, and John P. Conrad, "The Incapacitation of the Dangerous Offender: A Statistical Experiment," *Journal of Research in Crime and Delinquency,* vol. 14, no. 1 (1977):27. Reprinted with permission.

[a]Of the twenty persons with multiple offenses, six each were convicted for robbery-assault offenses and with murder/manslaughter-assault offenses, five for murder/manslaughter-robbery offenses, and 1 offender for each of three combinations: murder/manslaughter-sex offenses, robbery-sex offenses, assault-sex offenses.

[b]The twenty offenders convicted on multiple offenses generated fifty-seven conviction-counts, of which there were fourteen murder conviction-counts, twenty robbery conviction-counts, five sex offense conviction-counts, and eighteen assault conviction-counts.

percent of these crimes finally resulted in a conviction. There was the usual variation in clearance rates. Clearance by arrest for murder/manslaughter amounted to 95.4 percent and by conviction to 52.3 percent; this compares with national clearances for these crimes for 1973 of 81.0 percent and 26.4 percent respectively. Clearance rates for Franklin County aggravated assaults were 11.5 percent by arrest and 5.1 percent by conviction. Although 43.9 percent of the violent sex offenses were cleared by arrest, only 8.9 percent resulted in convictions, which probably reflects the difficulty in prosecuting such cases to a conclusion.[6]

The Frequency of Prior Felony Convictions

In table 3-26, we summarize the adult felony records of the 342 cohort members, classifying the offenses by violent and nonviolent felony convictions. In this cohort, 110, or 32.2 percent had prior adult felony convictions, of which thirty-six were violent. Only four of the 342 had three previous violent felony convictions; only two more had two such convictions. The most felonious member of the cohort had three violent and three nonviolent convictions. Few of the 342 members of the cohort could have been incapacitated for the crimes

Table 3-25
Total Recorded Violent Offenses and Violent Offenses Cleared,
Franklin County, Ohio 1973

	Reported Violent UCR Crimes Franklin County, 1973[a]	Cleared by Arrest		Cleared by Conviction	
		Number	Percent of UCR	Number	Percent of UCR
Murder/manslaughter	65	62	95.4	34	52.3
Robbery	1,554	324	20.8	120	7.7
Sex offenses (violent)	326	143	43.9	29	8.9
Assault	947	109	11.5	48	5.1
Total	2,892	638	22.1	231	8.0

Source: Stephan Van Dine, Simon Dinitz, and John P. Conrad, "The Incapacitation of the Dangerous Offender: A Statistical Experiment," *Journal of Research in Crime and Delinquency,* vol. 14, no. 1 (1977):28. Reprinted with permission.
[a]UCR denotes Uniform Crime Reports.

they committed by an incapacitation policy focused on repetitive violence. Only six of the 342 (1.8 percent) had more than a single violent conviction. By imposing life time incapacitation on all thirty-six members with records of a violent conviction, 10.5 percent of the cohort would have been prevented from the commission of their 1973 crimes. A policy of incapacitating all persons with any felony record would have reached 110 persons—32.2 percent of the cohort.

It is important to note that the average interval between the 1973 offense and the immediately previous felony conviction was 5.7 years, although the median interval was 3.6 years. Examining the interval between convictions of the

Table 3-26
Distribution by Number of Prior Violent and Nonviolent
Convictions of 342 Accused Adult Violent Offenders,
Franklin County, Ohio, 1973, Prior Adult Felony
Convictions Only

Number of Prior Non-Violent Convictions	Number of Prior Violent Convictions				Total
	0	1	2	3	
0	232	18	2	1	253
1	47	7	–	1	55
2	18	3	–	1	22
3	6	2	–	1	9
4	1	–	–	–	1
5	2	–	–	–	2
Total	306	30	2	4	342

110 recidivists, we found that an incapacitation period of three years would have prevented, at the most, only 42.8 percent of these persons from committing their 1973 offenses. With a five-year incapacitation, 64.6 percent of the recidivists might have been prevented from the commission of the 1973 violent offenses. (See table 3-27.)

Measuring the Effect of Incapacitation

Our most stringent sentencing policy, designated here as Policy 4, required that any person convicted of *any* felony, violent or not, would be sentenced to five full, or net, calendar years in prison. (None of our hypothetical policies allowed for early release for good time served, for parole, or for any modification of the sentence imposed except preconviction jail time.) We measured the effects of this policy using three different suppositions.

First, we assumed that the crimes on which the defendant was charged were correct and that he had been found guilty in every case. On that supposition, we found that at least 111 violent crimes of the 2,892 reported in 1973 would have been prevented by the five-year sentence. That was a reduction of 3.8 percent in the volume of violent crime. (See table 3-28.) These crimes were committed by 63 persons. Obviously, an unknown and unknowable fraction of the total number of crimes reported would have been prevented by the incarceration of these 63 offenders; the 111 crimes with which they were charged constitute the verified minimum number for which they were responsible. But there were 279 persons left in the cohort of 342 who could not have been prevented from committing either the crimes with which they were charged or those which they committed but on which they were not charged by the police. Whatever the

Table 3-27
Interval Between Prior Adult Felony Conviction and 1973 Offense for 110 Arrestees[a]

Length of Interval	Number	Percent
Less than 1 year	10	9.1
1-2 years	19	17.3
2-3 years	18	16.4
3-4 years	11	10.0
4-5 years	13	11.8
5-6 years	8	7.3
6-10 years	12	10.9
10-15 years	14	12.7
15 or more years	5	4.5
Total	110	100.0

[a]An additional 232 members of the cohort had no prior felony convictions.

Table 3-28
Summary of the Impact of Five Sentencing Policies

	Measure of Prevention					
Sentencing Policy Number	Persons Prevented	Percent of Cohort[a]	Indictment Charges Prevented	Percent of UCR[b]	Conviction Counts Prevented	Percent of UCR[b]
1	37	10.8	61	2.1	24	0.8
4	63	18.4	111	3.8	48	1.7
5	24	7.0	38	1.3	13	0.4
6	9	2.6	17	0.6	4	0.1
10	20	5.8	37	1.3	24	0.8

[a]The cohort consisted of 342 indictees.
[b]There was a total of 2,892 violent felonies in Franklin County in 1973.
Policy 1: One conviction, no prior violent felony, three-year mandatory sentence.
Policy 4: One conviction, no prior violent felony, five-year mandatory sentence.
Policy 5: Two convictions, no prior violent felony, five-year mandatory sentence.
Policy 6: Three convictions, no prior violent felony, five-year mandatory sentence.
Policy 10: One conviction, one violent felony required, five-year mandatory sentence.

total number of crimes these 279 persons actually committed, none could have been prevented by an incapacitating sentence because none of them had been convicted on a felony charge during the previous five years.

Second, we tried the cohort out on a more restrictive measure. We proceeded on the supposition that we could be certain a crime was prevented only if the person charged was found guilty of the crime. Obviously this is a more restrictive supposition than the one above, where we assumed that arrest implied guilt. By this yardstick, only forty-eight of the 2,892 (or 1.7 percent) crimes committed in 1973 would have been prevented. These forty-eight crimes were committed by thirty-six persons. Again, it is reasonable to suppose that these thirty-six persons must have been responsible for more than the forty-eight counts with which they were charged in 1973, but we cannot know how many more.

Third, we noted that of the 342 persons charged, sixty-three could have been prevented from the commission of whatever crimes they committed. That meant that a policy of incapacitation for five years would have reduced the number of persons charged in 1973 by 18.4 percent. The 111 crimes they committed constituted 17.4 percent of the 638 offenses with which our cohort of 342 was charged.

These three measures reflected various ways of calculating the reduction of crime attributable to an incapacitating sentence of five years imposed on all persons in the group who had been guilty of a previous felony during the period 1968-1973. We concluded that these results did not justify the extraordinarily severe sentencing policy on which the experiment was based.

These findings are well within the ranges suggested by the models proposed by Clarke, Greenberg, and Ehrlich. The Shinnars' estimate cannot be reconciled with our findings, even though this sentencing policy is more severe than any policy they suggest.

Policy 5 also calls for a mandatory sentence of five years, but it focuses on recidivist offenders. It is the most severe sentence applicable only to recidivists among the policies considered here.

Under this policy, twenty-four of the 342 indictees, charged with thirty-eight violent offenses, would have been prevented from committing these offenses in 1973 if this sentencing policy had been in effect. The percentage of Franklin County violent crime would have been reduced by 1.3 percent, using the arrest assumption. Using the population assumption, the reduction was 7.0 percent, while the reduction was a minute 0.4 percent under the conviction assumption.

The results of various sentencing policies (Policies 1, 4, 5, 6, and 10) are shown in table 3-28. It is apparent that none of these variants on the severe sentencing policy of Policy 4 would have prevented as great a proportion as of violent crime as our most drastic sentencing policy would have averted. But if Policy 4 were mandated by the statutes, every felon would serve a five-year sentence, even if the offense involved nothing more serious than bad checks, larceny, or auto theft. The absurd results to which such a policy would lead are hardly offset by the preventive effect described here. But any more specific policy would be even less effective in the prevention of violent crime. (See tables 3-29 to 3-44.)

The Failure of Incapacitation to Prevent Crime

Why doesn't incapacitation prevent more crime? This analysis suggests three reasons. First, our initial study did not assume the incapacitation of juveniles. Since in 1973 about one-fourth the persons arrested for violent crimes were juveniles,[7] stiffer policies that leave the juvenile system unaffected can have no impact on the incidence of juvenile violence. Certainly incapacitation of juvenile felony offenders would have prevented some violent crimes. Incapacitation policies applied to juvenile offenders would require a drastic modification of juvenile court legislation and the disposition of juvenile offenders.

Second, at least according to this study, the pool of violent recidivists that would have been immobilized through incapacitation is comparatively small in comparison to all those indicted for violent offenses. *Over two-thirds of the persons in this study were first-time felony offenders. Incapacitation could not have prevented their 1973 crimes.* Only 32 percent of the cohort had any previous felony conviction. Only 11 percent of the cohort, thirty-six of 342, had any previous *violent* felony conviction. (See table 3-26.) Thirteen percent of the

Table 3-29
The Impact of Policy 1 on the Amount of Crime Prevented, Arrest Level, and Conviction Level, Adult Records Only[a]

	Persons Indicted	Persons Prevented		1973 Violent UCR Crimes	Counts Prevented			
					Arrest Level		Conviction Level	
		Number	Percent of Indicted		Number	Percent of UCR	Number	Percent of UCR
Murder/manslaughter	36	5	13.9	65	12	18.5	7	10.8
Robbery	128	24	18.8	1554	43	2.8	15	1.0
Sex offenses (violent)	79	2	2.5	326	3	0.9	–	–
Assault	49	1	2.0	927	3	0.3	2	0.2
Multiple offenses (two of the above)	50	5	10.0	–	–	–	–	–
Total	342	37	10.8	2892	61	2.1	24	0.8

[a]Policy 1: A three-year net prison term imposed at the first felony conviction; no violent felonies are required.

Table 3-30
The Impact of Policy 2 on the Amount of Crime Prevented, Arrest Level, and Conviction Level, Adult Records Only[a]

	Persons Indicted	Persons Prevented		1973 Violent UCR Crimes	Counts Prevented			
					Arrest Level		Conviction Level	
		Number	Percent of Indicted		Number	Percent of UCR	Number	Percent of UCR
Murder/manslaughter	36	–	–	65	–	–	–	–
Robbery	128	11	8.6	1554	16	1.0	3	0.2
Sex offenses (violent)	79	2	2.5	326	3	0.9	–	–
Assault	49	–	–	927	1	0.1	1	0.1
Multiple offenses (two of the above)	50	2	4.0	–	–	–	–	–
Total	342	15	4.4	2892	20	0.7	4	0.1

[a]Policy 2: A three-year net prison term imposed after any second felony conviction; no violent felonies are required.

Table 3-31
The Impact of Policy 3 on the Amount of Crime Prevented, Arrest Level, and Conviction Level, Adult Records Only[a]

| | | | | Counts Prevented | | | |
| | Persons Prevented | | | Arrest Level | | Conviction Level | |
	Persons Indicted	Number	Percent of Indicted	1973 Violent UCR Crimes	Number	Percent of UCR	Number	Percent of UCR
Murder/manslaughter	36	–	–	65	–	–	–	–
Robbery	128	4	3.1	1554	9	0.6	2	0.1
Sex offenses (violent)	79	1	1.3	326	2	0.6	1	–
Assault	49	–	–	927	1	0.1	1	0.1
Multiple offenses (two of the above)	50	2	4.0	–	–	–	–	–
Total	342	7	2.0	2892	12	0.4	3	0.1

[a]Policy 3: A three-year net prison term imposed after any third felony conviction; no violent felonies are required.

Table 3-32
The Impact of Policy 4 on the Amount of Crime Prevented, Arrest Level, and Conviction Level, Adult Records Only[a]

	Persons Arrested	Persons Prevented		1973 Violent UCR Crimes	Counts Prevented			
					Arrest Level		Conviction Level	
		Number	Percent of Arrested		Number	Percent of UCR	Number	Percent of UCR
Murder/manslaughter	36	8	22.2	65	18	27.7	9	13.8
Robbery	128	35	27.3	1554	65	4.2	28	1.8
Sex offenses (violent)	79	7	10.1	326	22	6.7	5	1.5
Assault	49	1	2.0	927	6	0.6	6	0.6
Multiple offenses (two of the above)	50	11	22.0	—	—	—	—	—
Total	342	63	18.4	2892	111	3.8	48	1.7

[a]Policy 4: A five-year net prison term imposed at the first felony conviction; no violent felonies are required.

Table 3-33
The Impact of Policy 5 on the Amount of Crime Prevented, Arrest Level, and Conviction Level, Adult Records Only[a]

	Persons Indicted	Persons Prevented		1973 Violent UCR Crimes	Counts Prevented			
					Arrest Level		Conviction Level	
		Number	Percent of Indicted		Number	Percent of UCR	Number	Percent of UCR
Murder/manslaughter	36	–	–	65	2	3.1	1	1.5
Robbery	128	16	12.5	1554	26	1.7	10	0.6
Sex offenses (violent)	79	5	6.3	326	8	2.5	–	–
Assault	49	–	–	927	2	0.2	2	0.2
Multiple offenses (two of the above)	50	3	6.0	–	–	–	–	–
Total	342	24	7.0	2892	38	1.3	13	0.4

aPolicy 5: A five-year net prison term imposed after any second felony conviction; no violent felonies are required.

Table 3-34
The Impact of Policy 6 on the Amount of Crime Prevented, Arrest Level, and Conviction Level, Adult Records Only[a]

| | | Persons Prevented | | | Counts Prevented | | | |
| | | | | | Arrest Level | | Conviction Level | |
	Persons Indicted	Number	Percent of Indicted	1973 Violent UCR Crimes	Number	Percent of UCR	Number	Percent of UCR
Murder/manslaughter	36	–	–	65	–	–	–	–
Robbery	128	5	3.9	1554	11	0.7	3	0.2
Sex offenses (violent)	79	2	2.5	326	5	1.5	–	–
Assault	49	–	–	927	1	0.1	1	0.1
Multiple offenses (two of the above)	50	2	4.0	–	–	–	–	–
Total	342	9	2.6	2892	17	0.6	4	0.1

aPolicy 6: A five-year net prison term imposed after any third felony conviction; no violent felonies are required.

Table 3-35
The Impact of Policy 7 on the Amount of Crime Prevented, Arrest Level, and Conviction Level, Adult Records Only[a]

| | Persons Indicted | Persons Prevented | | 1973 Violent UCR Crimes | Counts Prevented | | | |
| | | | | | Arrest Level | | Conviction Level | |
		Number	Percent of Indicted		Number	Percent of UCR	Number	Percent of UCR
Murder/manslaughter	36	1	2.8	65	2	3.1	2	3.1
Robbery	128	6	4.7	1554	7	0.5	5	0.3
Sex offenses (violent)	79	1	1.3	326	1	0.3	–	–
Assault	49	–	–	927	1	0.1	1	0.1
Multiple offenses (two of the above)	50	1	2.0	–	–	–	–	–
Total	342	9	2.6	2892	11	0.4	8	0.3

aPolicy 7: A three-year net prison term imposed after any first felony conviction; one violent felony is required.

Table 3-36
The Impact of Policy 8 on the Amount of Crime Prevented, Arrest Level, and Conviction Level, Adult Records Only[a]

	Persons Indicted	Persons Prevented		1973 Violent UCR Crimes	Counts Prevented			
					Arrest Level		Conviction Level	
		Number	Percent of Indicted		Number	Percent of UCR	Number	Percent of UCR
Murder/manslaughter	36	–	–	65	–	–	–	–
Robbery	128	3	2.3	1554	4	0.3	3	0.2
Sex offenses (violent)	79	1	1.3	326	1	0.3	–	–
Assault	49	–	–	927	1	0.1	1	0.1
Multiple offenses (two of the above)	50	1	2.0	–	–	–	–	–
Total	342	5	1.5	2892	6	0.2	4	0.1

[a]Policy 8: A three-year net prison term imposed after any second felony conviction, one violent felony is required.

Table 3-37
The Impact of Policy 9 on the Amount of Crime Prevented, Arrest Level, and Conviction Level, Adult Records Only[a]

| | Persons Indicted | Persons Prevented | | 1973 Violent UCR Crimes | Counts Prevented | | | |
| | | | | | Arrest Level | | Conviction Level | |
		Number	Percent of Indicted		Number	Percent of UCR	Number	Percent of UCR
Murder/manslaughter	36	–	–	65	–	–	–	–
Robbery	128	2	1.6	1554	3	0.2	2	0.1
Sex offenses (violent)	79	1	1.3	326	1	0.3	–	–
Assault	49	–	–	927	1	0.1	1	0.1
Multiple offenses (two of the above)	50	1	2.0	–	–	–	–	–
Total	342	4	1.2	2892	5	0.2	3	0.1

[a]Policy 9: A three-year net prison term imposed after any third felony conviction; one violent felony is required.

Table 3-38
The Impact of Policy 10 on the Amount of Crime Prevented, Arrest Level, and Conviction Level, Adult Records Only[a]

| | Persons Prevented | | 1973 Violent UCR Crimes | Counts Prevented | | | |
| | | | | Arrest Level | | Conviction Level | |
Persons Indicted	Number	Percent of Indicted		Number	Percent of UCR	Number	Percent of UCR
Murder/manslaughter	36	2	5.6	65	5	7.7	3	4.6
Robbery	128	10	7.8	1554	17	1.1	13	0.8
Sex offenses (violent)	79	3	3.8	326	11	3.4	3	0.9
Assault	49	–	–	927	4	0.4	5	0.5
Multiple offenses (two of the above)	50	5	10.0	–	–	–	–	–
Total	342	20	5.8	2892	37	1.3	24	0.8

aPolicy 10: A five-year net prison term imposed after any first felony conviction; one violent felony is required.

Table 3-39
The Impact of Policy 11 on the Amount of Crime Prevented, Arrest Level, and Conviction Level, Adult Records Only[a]

	Persons Indicted	Persons Prevented		1973 Violent UCR Crimes	Counts Prevented			
					Arrest Level		Conviction Level	
		Number	Percent of Indicted		Number	Percent of UCR	Number	Percent of UCR
Murder/manslaughter	36	–	–	65	2	3.1	1	1.5
Robbery	128	5	3.9	1554	10	0.6	9	0.6
Sex offenses (violent)	79	2	2.5	326	2	0.6	–	–
Assault	49	–	–	927	2	0.2	2	0.2
Multiple offenses (two of the above)	50	2	4.0	–	–	–	–	–
Total	342	9	2.6	2892	16	0.6	12	0.4

aPolicy 11: A five-year net prison term imposed after any second felony conviction; one violent felony is required.

Table 3-40
The Impact of Policy 12 on the Amount of Crime Prevented, Arrest Level, and Conviction Level, Adult Records Only[a]

	Persons Indicted	Persons Prevented		1973 Violent UCR Crimes	Counts Prevented			
					Arrest Level		Conviction Level	
		Number	Percent of Indicted		Number	Percent of UCR	Number	Percent of UCR
Murder/manslaughter	36	–	–	65	–	–	–	–
Robbery	128	2	1.6	1554	3	0.2	2	0.1
Sex offenses (violent)	79	1	1.3	326	1	0.3	–	–
Assault	49	–	–	927	1	0.1	1	0.1
Multiple offenses (two of the above)	50	1	2.0	–	–	–	–	–
Total	342	4	1.2	2892	5	0.2	3	0.1

[a]Policy 12: A five-year net prison term imposed after any third felony conviction; one violent felony is required.

Table 3-41
The Impact of Policy 14 on the Amount of Crime Prevented, Arrest Level, and Conviction Level, Adult Records Only[a]

| | Persons Indicted | Persons Prevented | | 1973 Violent UCR Crimes | Counts Prevented | | | |
| | | | | | Arrest Level | | Conviction Level | |
		Number	Percent of Indicted		Number	Percent of UCR	Number	Percent of UCR
Murder/manslaughter	36	—	—	65	—	—	—	—
Robbery	128	1	0.8	1554	2	0.1	1	0.1
Sex offenses (violent)	79	—	—	326	1	0.1	—	—
Assault	49	—	—	927	1	0.1	—	—
Multiple offenses (two of the above)	50	1	2.0	—	—	—	—	—
Total	342	2	0.6	2892	3	0.1	1	0.0

aPolicy 14: Three-year net prison term imposed after any second felony conviction; two violent felonies are required.

Table 3-42
The Impact of Policy 15 on the Amount of Crime Prevented, Arrest Level, and Conviction Level, Adult Records Only[a]

	Persons Indicted	Persons Prevented		1973 Violent UCR Crimes	Counts Prevented			
					Arrest Level		Conviction Level	
		Number	Percent of Indicted		Number	Percent of UCR	Number	Percent of UCR
Murder/manslaughter	36	–	–	65	–	–	–	–
Robbery	128	1	0.8	1554	2	0.1	1	0.1
Sex offenses (violent)	79	–	–	326	–	–	–	–
Assault	49	–	–	927	1	0.1	–	–
Multiple offenses (two of the above)	50	1	2.0	–	–	–	–	–
Total	342	2	0.6	2892	3	0.1	1	0.0

aPolicy 15: A three-year net prison term imposed after any third felony conviction; two violent felonies are required.

Table 3-43
The Impact of Policy 17 on the Amount of Crime Prevented, Arrest Level, and Conviction Level, Adult Records Only[a]

| | Persons Indicted | Persons Prevented | | 1973 Violent UCR Crimes | Counts Prevented | | | |
| | | | | | Arrest Level | | Conviction Level | |
		Number	Percent of Indicted		Number	Percent of UCR	Number	Percent of UCR
Murder/manslaughter	36	–	–	65	–	–	–	–
Robbery	128	1	0.8	1554	2	0.1	1	0.1
Sex offenses (violent)	79	–	–	326	–	–	1	–
Assault	49	–	–	927	1	0.1	–	–
Multiple offenses (two of the above)	50	1	2.0	–	–	–	–	–
Total	342	2	0.6	2892	3	0.1	1	0.0

aPolicy 17: A five-year net prison term imposed after any second felony conviction; two violent felonies are required.

Table 3-44
The Impact of Policy 18 on the Amount of Crime Prevented, Arrest Level, and Conviction Level, Adult Records Only[a]

| | | Persons Prevented | | | Counts Prevented | | | |
| | | | | | Arrest Level | | Conviction Level | |
	Persons Indicted	Number	Percent of Indicted	1973 Violent UCR Crimes	Number	Percent of UCR	Number	Percent of UCR
Murder/manslaughter	36	—	—	65	—	—	—	—
Robbery	128	1	0.8	1554	2	0.1	1	0.1
Sex offenses (violent)	79	—	—	326	—	—	—	—
Assault	49	—	—	927	1	0.1	—	—
Multiple offenses (two of the above)	50	1	2.0	—	—	—	—	—
Total	342	2	0.6	2892	3	0.1	1	0.0

aPolicy 18: A five-year net prison term imposed after any third felony conviction; two violent felonies are required.

cohort had two or more felonies of any type. The potential target groups are too small for incapacitation to be truly effective.

Third, the rate of repetition for the recidivist group is too low to provide significant reductions in the incidence of crime through an incapacitation policy. The average interval between violent incidents for a repeat offender was 5.6 years; the median was 3.6 years. Probably some of this delay was caused by difficulties in apprehending an offender after his return to crime. Nonetheless, the typical offender in this cohort probably committed violent crime infrequently; at the least he was arrested infrequently. The clearest example is the case of the most frequent offender. This man had six prior felony offenses and was convicted in 1973 of a seventh. Yet it took him forty years to acquire such a record. Two persons had five convictions; one began his felony career in 1937, the other in 1945. The implication is that while career violent offenders may commit their crimes persistently, they do so slowly.

Only 30 percent of Columbus' reported violent crime was cleared in 1973 by an adult or juvenile arrest. The Shinnars premise their study on the belief that most uncleared crime is committed by those arrested. Following these writers, a strict incapacitation policy would prevent far more crime than is actually cleared by arrest. Our analysis suggests that this assumption is generally in error, and certainly inaccurate at a level necessary to support the Shinnars' conclusions.

For incapacitation to be effective, two conditions must exist. First, the apprehension rate must be greatly increased, unless it can be shown that a very large percentage of uncleared crimes are committed by those who are arrested. Second, a large percentage of crimes must be committed by repeat offenders, much higher than has been found in this study. This second condition depends upon the assumption that convicted offenders spend very little time in prison. Advocates of an incapacitation policy assume that both of these conditions are largely true. These results suggest that they are not.

Effect of Incapacitating Adults with Juvenile Records

So far, our sights have been trained on the effectiveness of various policies of incapacitation of adult offenders in reducing the incidence of violent crime. We have noted that one of the reasons for the limited usefulness of such policies might be the exclusion of the juvenile records from the cohort analysis. In chapter 4 we shall consider the effectiveness of various incarcerative policies in reducing the rate of violent crime committed by juveniles.

Before discussing juveniles we need to consider the impact on our population of 342 adult offenders if incapacitation was imposed on juveniles and if juvenile records were used in the adult system. There would be two effects. First, many of the young adult offenders might have been incarcerated on a juvenile offense if extended incapacitation were imposed in the juvenile system.

Second, many of the sentencing policies require more than a single felony before incapacitative sentences would be imposed. As we have seen, few adults have multiple felony convictions. By including juvenile felony convictions, the impact of many of the more restrictive policies is increased.

Our question at this point is: If the various incapacitation policies had been imposed across both juvenile and adult felony records, how many more of the 342 cohort members would have been prevented from committing their 1973 offense?

To arrive at an answer to this question, we extended our record-gathering to the juvenile files of the Columbus Police Department. We were then able to supplement this search with the records of the Ohio Youth Commission.

About three-fourths (or 254) of the cohort had a Columbus background. The rest had either lived elsewhere as juveniles, or the record was blank as to early residence. For offenders older than twenty-three at the time of the 1973 charge, a record of youthful criminality in any jurisdiction would be irrelevant for the purposes of this study. For the young adult offender between eighteen and twenty-three, a five-year incapacitation sentence imposed anywhere would have prevented the 1973 Columbus offense. However, we doubt that our findings are seriously distorted by our inability to take this possibility into account.

Table 3-45 presents the felony records of the 342 adult offenders when both adult and juvenile convictions are included. Almost half, 161 of the cohort of 342, or 47.1 percent, now show felony conviction records. In the group thus expanded, sixteen (4.7 percent) had two or more violent felony convictions, and sixty-two (18.1 percent) had at least one such conviction. Collectively, the

Table 3-45

Distribution by Number of Prior Violent and Nonviolent Convictions of 342 Accused Adult Violent Offenders, Franklin County, Ohio, 1973, Prior Adult and Juvenile Felonies

Number of Prior Non-Violent Convictions	Number of Prior Violent Convictions				
	0	1	2	3	Total
0	181	15	3	1	200
1	41	7	1	1	50
2	32	8	3	1	44
3	12	9	2	2	25
4	7	2	1	1	11
5	3	3	—	—	6
6	2	1	—	—	3
7	1	1	—	—	2
8	1	—	—	—	1
Total	280	46	10	6	342

cohort had 186 adult felony convictions, but there were 225 juvenile convictions on their records. Table 3-46 presents the increased incapacitating effect produced by applying Policy 4 to the 342 while juvenile or adult. If it is assumed that all arrests should have resulted in convictions, the number of persons thus incapacitated rises from sixty-three to ninety-three, from 18.4 to 27.2 percent of the cohort. This level of incapacitation would have prevented 175 offenses—or 6.1 percent of the 2,892 violent crimes reported. If Policy 4 is applied only to those convicted on the 1973 felony charge, only seventy-eight, or 2.7 percent of the reported offenses would have been prevented. Either way these results could only be achieved by drastic and costly changes in the criminal justice system, and by accepting a very large increase in the number of persons incarcerated. The assumptions of juvenile justice would have to be fundamentally changed.

The results of the five principal sentencing policies are displayed in table 3-47. Obviously none of the other policies are as effective as is Policy 4. Figure 3-1 illustrates the consequences of including the juvenile records when applying the policies.

In this figure, the lower, unshaded portion of each bar represents the percentage of the cohort that would have been prevented from committing the 1973 offense by a consideration of the adult record only. The shaded upper portion of the bar represents the fraction of the 342 cohort members whose crimes would have been prevented if juvenile felony records could have been used as a basis for the sentence. Note that while for Policy 4 the number of offenders incapacitated would have been far greater than for any other policy, the increase in incapacitation is proportionately far greater in Policies 5 and 6 when juvenile records are considered. More crime is prevented when juveniles are incapacitated like adults. Why? Is it because juveniles receive much shorter sentences—or no sentences at all? Or is it because the juvenile records of young adult offenders have been sealed? The answers are to be found in the application of the policies to the new information gained from inspection of the juvenile records for this study.

As expected, the thirty individuals whose offenses would have been prevented by the application of Policy 4 had their most recent conviction while still juveniles. Under Policy 5, two recent felonies were required. Thirty-nine additional offenders had been incapacitated, of whom twenty-three had been most recently convicted as juveniles. The remaining sixteen persons had been incapacitated by a combination of one juvenile and one adult prior offense. In Policy 6, which required three previous felonies, only eight would still have been incarcerated because of juvenile offenses. The remainder, twenty-five offenders, would not have qualified for Policy 6 without the inclusion of both juvenile and adult convictions.

Figure 3-2 duplicates the results of figure 3-1, only the arrest assumption is used rather than focusing on the number of people. The proportions remain relatively the same across the five policies. In the most notable instance, Policy

Table 3-46
The Impact of Policy 4 on the Amount of Crime Prevented, Arrest Level, and Conviction Level, Adult Records and Juvenile Records[a]

| | Persons Arrested | Persons Prevented | | 1973 Violent UCR Crimes | Counts Prevented | | | |
| | | | | | Arrest Level | | Conviction Level | |
		Number	Percent of Arrested		Number	Percent of UCR	Number	Percent of UCR
Murder/manslaughter	36	11	30.6	65	21	32.3	12	18.5
Robbery	128	50	39.1	1554	104	6.7	45	2.9
Sex offenses (violent)	79	14	17.7	326	37	11.3	10	3.1
Assault	49	1	2.0	927	13	1.4	11	1.2
Multiple offenses (two of the above)	50	17	34.0	–	–	–	–	–
Total	342	93	27.2	2892	175	6.1	78	2.7

[a]Policy 4: A five-year net prison term imposed after any felony conviction; no violent felonies are required.

Table 3-47
**Summary of Impact of Five Sentencing Policies, Including
Juvenile Records**

Sentencing Policy Number[a]	Measure of Prevention					
	Persons Prevented	Percent of Cohort	Indictment Charges Prevented	Percent of UCR	Conviction Counts Prevented	Percent of UCR
1	50	14.6	86	3.0	36	1.2
4	93	27.2	175	6.1	78	2.7
5	63	18.4	121	4.2	49	1.7
6	42	12.3	71	2.5	30	1.0
10	38	11.1	67	2.3	39	1.3

[a]Policy 1: One conviction, no prior violent felony, three-year mandatory sentence.
Policy 4: One conviction, no prior violent felony, five-year mandatory sentence.
Policy 5: Two convictions, no prior violent felony, five-year mandatory sentence.
Policy 6: Three convictions, no prior violent felony, five-year mandatory sentence.
Policy 10: One conviction, one violent felony required, five-year mandatory sentence.

6, five times as many persons—and crimes—are prevented when juvenile offenses
are included as when they are not.

Conclusions

Surely all but a few citizens would agree that violent recidivists should be
subjected to protracted removal from the community. Opinions diverge, however, on the basis for which a recidivist ought to be imprisoned. Some argue that
repeat offenders are demonstrated threats to the community and should be put
away in defense of society. Others argue that punishment alone is a sufficient
basis for imprisonment of the repeat offender.

A third group has argued for the removal of the violent recidivist from the
community for the purpose of reducing crime through incapacitation. This study
has followed the arguments of those incapacitation advocates, investigating the
consequences when incapacitation is assigned the primary role in justifying
imprisonment. Our results disappoint the hopes of these advocates. It must not
be expected that a policy of incapacitation will result in a significant statistical
reduction in the rate of violent crime. Further, it is not reasonable to expect that
the public would tolerate, or the legislature would enact, statutes providing for a
flat five year prison term for a first conviction of auto theft, burglary or bad
checks. But that is what our sentencing Policy 4 calls for and we have seen the
impact that its application would have on the crime rate. If the country is
serious about the reduction of violent crime, other means for accomplishing this
goal will have to be sought.

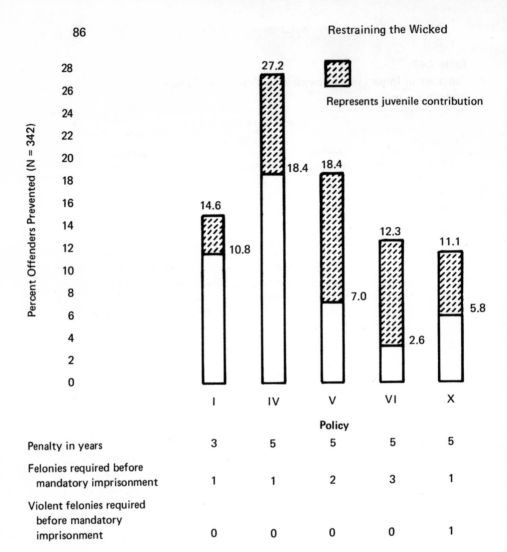

Figure 3-1. Violent Offenders Prevented From 1973 Crime by Five Sentencing
Policies, With and Without Juvenile Record

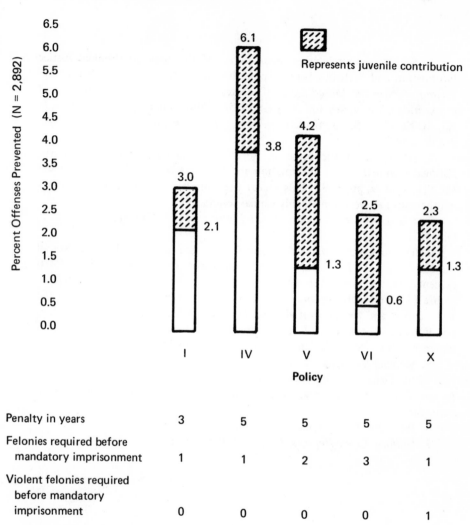

Figure 3-2. Percentage of UCR Crimes Prevented by Five Sentencing Policies, With and Without Juvenile Record

Notes

1. See the comprehensive report series of the National Criminal Justice Information and Statistics Service, published annually under the title *Criminal Victimization in the United States*. The latest issue available to us at the time of this writing is the survey for the year 1975, published in December 1977 under No. SD-NCS-N-7. See particularly p. 9, *Reporting Victimizations to the Police*, and the tables cited.

2. See Criminal Victimization Surveys in Cincinnati published by the National Criminal Justice Information and Statistics Service (July 1977) under No. SD-NCS-C-9, pp. 5, 33. This survey was completed in 1974. Similar surveys in other cities arrive at remarkably similar results.

3. *U.S. Census of Population and Housing: 1970–Columbus, Ohio*, p. 1, table P-1.

4. The cohort consists of all violent felony cases completed in 1973. Not all the cases began in 1973. Half the individuals were first booked in 1973 (50.0 percent), most of the rest in 1972 (45.6 percent) and the remainder in 1971 or before (4.4 percent). For simplicity in the study, the population is called the 1973 cohort and treated as if all cases began in 1973. This determination does not influence the results of the study, since the hypothetical incapacitation sentence is imposed on each person's record individually.

5. Stephan Van Dine, Simon Dinitz, and John P. Conrad, "The Incapacitation of the Dangerous Offender: A Statistical Experiment," *Journal of Research in Crime and Delinquency*, vol. 14, no. 1 (1977):24-25. Reprinted with permission.

6. Ibid., 26-28. Reprinted with permission.

7. *Uniform Crime Reports, 1973*, p. 130, table 31.

4 Can Incapacitation Prevent Juvenile Crime?

Our problem is to prevent violent crime, and juveniles commit about one-fourth of it. Aware of this statistic, many legislatures have enacted or are considering the enactment of statutes that will require much more rigorous control of violent juvenile offenders. The state of New York has passed into law legislation which lowers the age of criminal responsibility to thirteen for some offenses involving violence.[1] The obvious expectation is that the removal of such children from the community will reduce the incidence of violent crime by deterring many from committing it and incapacitating those who are not deterred. What can be expected from such a strategy?

The logic works as well with juveniles as it does with adults. Five years in custody will prevent a juvenile from committing a street crime in exactly the same way as such a term will prevent an adult offender from continuing his depredations. Such a term may not be a realistic disposition for either youthful or adult offenders, but as a statistical experiment we can find out what would have happened if, at the last previous felony conviction, a juvenile had been subjected to the sentencing options discussed in chapter 3 and applied to adult offenders. Once again we accept the limit imposed by our system of criminal justice: Neither adults or juveniles can be deprived of their freedom without conviction of a serious crime. The problem of making the punishment fit the risk of future crime is to be explored by an examination of the consequences of varying sentencing policies applied with a rigor never before administered in juvenile justice.

We undertook a study of the juveniles arrested by the Columbus police for violent crimes in 1973: These juvenile offenders committed their share of the 2,892 offenses which constituted the universe of violent crime known to the police in Franklin County during that year. However, we found it necessary to draw out data from the records of the Columbus police rather than from the Franklin County courts. That decision limited the universe we were exploring to the 2,622 crimes of violence reported in Columbus alone during that year.[2]

The exploration called for a search of the files to locate every person seventeen years old or younger in 1973 who was charged with a crime of violence in 1973 and then to determine which of them had previous felony convictions. That proved to be a laborious undertaking. Civilian employees of the police department examined the microfiche records of all juveniles who could conceivably have committed a violent crime in 1973. The main sources of information were contained in alphabetically filed folders in which police case record and investigative reports are stored. The system in use by the Columbus police is obviously efficient for maintaining a running record of the offenses committed by any juvenile in the course of his delinquent career, but it presents serious problems for the researcher trying to identify all those persons charged with certain specific crimes and only those persons. To enable the reader to understand what this search entailed, and to allow for the possibility of an understatement of the number of juveniles charged, we must outline here the filing procedures in use by the police.

When an arrest is first filed on a juvenile, a permanent identification number is assigned and a folder is established for that number, which is retained in numerical order. An alphabetical file is maintained with a card for each name and the number assigned. All subsequent arrest reports will be filed by identification number. As these numbers are assigned sequentially, the series for any year is continuous and its beginning and ending is readily ascertained. This system makes it impossible to determine who did what in any given year except by folder-by-folder search. To locate all youths arrested for a 1973 violent crime, we had to search all folders beginning with those opened in 1961, the year when the eighteen-year-olds of 1973 were six. All we needed was the arrest reports of 1973 in which a violent crime was charged, but even with microfiche technology, sorting the needles from the hay was a task of considerable magnitude.

The search yielded 126 cases in which a juvenile had been arrested for a violent crime in that year—125 boys and one girl. Because many hundreds of files had to be reviewed to obtain this total, the possibility of error by understatement exists; we cannot be as sure of the cohort's completeness as we are in the adult cohort. We consider it unlikely that more than a handful of cases were missed. We are confident of the representative nature of the 126 cases we are about to consider.

The Violent Juveniles in 1973

As would be expected, the demographic data for the juvenile cohort was closely congruent with the adult cohort. There were seventy-one blacks and fifty-five whites (the latter figure including the lone female), with percentages of 56.3 and 43.7. (See table 4-1.)

As to socioeconomic status, the same review of residence address resulted in a distribution of the cohort by census tract, for each of which the median income was ascertained. The vast majority, 82.5 percent, lived in tracts with median incomes below the median for the city. (See table 4-2.) Like their adult counterparts, these juveniles were poor, almost exclusively male, and disproportionately black. About half were under sixteen when arrested; the youngest was nine, and seven were under thirteen. (See table 4-3.)

Table 4-1
Race and Sex Distribution of Violent Juveniles

Category Label	Number	Percent
Black male	71	56.3
White male	54	42.9
Black female	0	0.0
White female	1	0.8
Total	126	100.0

Eighty-five of our 126 violent juveniles had no previous criminal record. The remaining forty-one subjects had between one and nine prior police contacts for a grand total of eighty-three felony arrests. Table 4-4 recapitulates the prior offenses in detail. It must be stressed that it does not include multiple and concurrent charges included in the same arrest. Of these forty-one second offenders, twenty-one went on to be charged with a second offense. There were only two chronic offenders, persons charged with five or more offenses.

Most of the prior arrests were for property offenses. Thirty-six of the eighty-three charges against our juvenile recidivists were for some form of burglary; the second most frequent offense category was auto theft, with eighteen. Crimes against the person were much less frequent; there were nine unarmed robberies and a scattering of the other violent offenses. Certainly these data give us no base for predicting the commission of a violent offense in 1973.

Only forty-one of our cohort of 126 were recidivists. It must be borne in mind that these young people do not represent completed criminal careers. Many of the eighty-five single offenders must be individuals who will go on to subsequent offenses, a speculation which is supported by the distribution of the cohort by age. But of the forty-one recidivists, twenty-one had a second arrest and ten had a third. (See table 4-5.) Allowing for the arbitrary termination of a delinquent career at age eighteen, it is likely that the indicated rate of desistance understates the drift into continuing criminality.

Table 4-2
Residence of Violent Juveniles by Trace Income

Median Income Category	Number	Percent
Below $5,291	9	7.1
$5,292 to $8,465	43	34.1
$8,466 to $10,582	52	41.3
Above $10,582	18	14.3
Unknown	4	3.2
Total	126	100.0

Table 4-3
Age of 126 Juveniles at Arrest for Violent Crime in 1973

Age	Number	Percent
9	1	0.8
10	1	0.8
11	1	0.8
12	4	3.2
13	12	9.5
14	24	19.0
15	23	18.3
16	30	23.8
17	30	23.8
Total	126	100.0

Of the eighty-three charges against the entire cohort, sixty-four resulted in conviction of a felony offense. Table 4-6 displays the outcomes: One quarter of the cases resulted in a commitment to the Ohio Youth Commission; another half of the group of cases, forty-two in number, resulted in an informal finding of guilt or probation.

These forty-two cases require special attention. Procedures for establishing guilt in the juvenile system during this period were often casual. There was no special penalty to a determination of guilty when the court knew that the

Table 4-4
Types of Prior Offenses Charged to 126 Violent Juveniles

Offense Type	Offense Sequence Number									Total
	1	2	3	4	5	6	7	8	9	
Armed robbery	–	–	1	–	–	–	–	–	–	1
Rape	1	–	1	–	–	–	–	–	–	2
Unarmed robbery	6	2	–	1	–	–	–	–	–	9
Assault to rape	–	2	–	–	–	–	–	–	–	2
Assault to rob	1	–	1	–	–	–	–	–	–	2
Aggravated assault	1	–	–	–	–	–	–	–	–	1
Burglary	2	–	1	–	1	1	–	–	–	5
Breaking and entering	14	9	4	1	–	–	–	–	–	28
Breaking and entering at night	2	1	–	–	–	–	–	–	–	3
Receiving and concealing	1	1	–	–	–	–	–	–	–	2
Possession criminal tools	1	–	–	–	–	–	–	–	–	1
Auto theft	3	4	1	1	1	1	–	–	–	11
Operating motor vehicle without owner's concent	4	–	–	1	–	–	1	1	–	7
Carry concealed weapon	1	1	–	–	–	–	–	–	–	2
Larceny	2	1	1	–	–	–	–	–	1	5
Attempt burn property	2	–	–	–	–	–	–	–	–	2
Total	41	21	10	4	2	2	1	1	1	83

Table 4-5
Persistence and Desistance from Additional Offenses of Cases with Prior Records

Prior Arrests	Number of Cases	Percent Persistence	Number of Desistors
1	41	—	—
2	21	51.2	20
3	10	47.6	11
4	4	40.0	6
5	2	50.0	2
6	2	100.0	0
7	1	50.0	1
8	1	100.0	0
9	1	100.0	0

punishment would be an oral rebuke before sending the youth home (generally summarized as "reprimand and release"). Thus, the guilty verdict in these forty-two cases counts as a conviction that would probably not be sustained if the consequences were more serious (for example, if they resulted in mandatory imprisonment). The use of these "soft" convictions overstates the effectiveness of incapacitation if imposed on juveniles.

Offenses, Findings, and Dispositions

Table 4-7 shows the distribution of the 1973 juvenile offenders by most serious offense. Table 4-8 follows with the total number of violent crimes, by type, charged to these offenders. It must be stressed, again, that this listing does not include all the crimes committed in 1973 by our cohort and known to the police. Neither the police nor the juvenile court use the formal charging procedures for juveniles that are customary when they are dealing with adults; only the most serious offense is charged. It is certain that many more offenses

Table 4-6
Disposition for Eighty-three Prior Felony Arrests Committed by Juveniles

Disposition	Number	Percent
Convicted, to youth commission	22	26.5
Convicted, informal release and probation	42	50.6
Not guilty	16	19.3
Unknown	3	3.6
Total	83	100.0

Table 4-7
Distribution of 1973 Juvenile Offenders by Most Serious Offense

Category Label	Number of Offenders	Percent
Murder I	1	0.8
Armed robbery	24	19.0
Rape	9	7.1
Unarmed robbery	59	46.8
Manslaughter I	1	0.8
Sodomy	7	5.6
Assault to rape	1	0.8
Assault to rob	6	4.8
Aggravated assault	18	14.3
Total	126	100.0

were committed than are listed here, but we cannot even say how many were violent. We do know that there were 154 charges of violent crime standing against our 126 youths, of which 111 were robberies, but we have no reason to doubt that there were more such crimes committed and known to the police, but on which no formal charge was made. The minimum figure presented in table 4-8 results in 5.9 percent of the 2,622 violent crimes reported to the Columbus police in 1973 being cleared by the arrest of a juvenile. Only 106, or 4.0 percent resulted in clearance by conviction.

Juvenile court jurisdiction was waived for only one of the juveniles. Of the 96 individuals actually found guilty, twenty-eight, or 29.2 percent were committed to a facility of the Ohio Youth Commission. One boy went to a reformatory; three received jail sentences, and most of the rest were managed in the community. These dispositions are displayed in table 4-9. Without more particulars than we have on the nature of the offenses committed by these

Table 4-8
Violent Offenses Cleared by Juvenile Arrest and by Juvenile Conviction in 1973

Violent UCR Crimes, Columbus, Ohio, 1973[a]	Number Reported	Cleared by Arrest		Cleared by Conviction	
		Number	Percent of UCR	Number	Percent of UCR
Murder/manslaughter	64	2	3.1	1	1.6
Robbery	1508	111	7.4	74	4.9
Sex offenses (violent)	295	18	6.1	11	3.7
Assault	755	23	3.0	20	2.6
Total	2622	154	5.9	106	4.0

[a]Uniform Crime Reports, table 75, p. 223.

Table 4-9
Sanction Imposed in Instant Offense

Category Label	Number	Percent	Percent of Guilty
Not guilty	30	23.8	—
Fine or restitution	1	0.8	1.0
Jail	3	2.4	3.1
Probation	18	14.3	18.7
Prison	1	0.8	1.0
Referral	13	10.3	13.4
Reprimand	10	7.9	10.4
Suspended, Ohio Youth Commission	2	1.6	2.1
Detention	7	5.6	7.3
Ohio Youth Commission	28	22.2	29.2
Informal	1	0.8	1.0
Hold open for investigation	7	5.6	7.3
Detention suspended	2	1.6	2.1
Detention plus fine or restitution	1	0.8	1.0
Detention plus probation	2	1.6	2.1
Total[a]	126	100.1	99.7

[a]Errors are due to rounding.

young people, it is difficult to evaluate the appropriateness of the juvenile court's response in committing 33.2 percent of those found guilty to various incarcerative facilities. It is clear that whether or not the court correctly evaluated the youths who appeared before it on charges of violent offenses, about two-thirds did not appear to require an incapacitating disposition. But if the courts of Franklin County were persuaded of the need for a strategy of severe restraint of violent juvenile offenders, it would be expected that the severity would begin with our cohort of 126. Obviously that policy did not appear to be justified in 1973.

The Effectiveness of the Incapacitation of Juveniles

The sentencing options that were investigated for adult offenders in the previous chapter are, for the most part, more severe than are generally administered anywhere in the country. They are even more incongruous when we think of applying them to juveniles. Ingrained in the national value system is the view that juveniles in any kind of trouble are to be helped to the extent that help can be given. The artificial barriers set up between adult and juvenile offenders result in some arbitrary anomalies. Immature young men of nineteen or twenty are packed off to prisons and "reformatories" who ought to be in youth-training facilities, whereas some very tough sixteen- and seventeen-year-olds are kept in juvenile facilities where the authorities are hard-pressed to contain them.

Nevertheless, the barrier exists for a well-defined public purpose; the criminal justice system is kept on notice that children are to be treated as children no matter how grave the damage they may do to others and to the community. That barrier may be eroding, as we have seen in the enactment of increasingly stringent legislation against violent youthful offenders, but it must be removed entirely before an across-the-board policy of incapacitation can be a reality.

The adoption of such a policy will have limited value if its main objective is the reduction of violent crime. Using the total of 2,622 violent crimes reported to the Columbus police in 1973 as our denominator, we tested the effectiveness of each of the sixteen sentencing policies listed in table 4-10 to determine the number of juveniles who would have been prevented from the commission of their 1973 offenses. The strongest medicine, sentencing Policy 4, calling for a five year incapacitating term for the conviction of *any* felony, is even more unreasonable when considered for juveniles than it would be for adults. Of our cohort of 126, thirty-three (26.2 percent) would have been prevented from their 1973 crimes had such a sentencing policy prevailed during the previous five years. The significance of this percentage may be open to some debate. After all, to prevent thirty-three individuals from committing thirty-five serious offenses is not an inconsiderable gain, especially to the victims of those offenses. But only

Table 4-10
The Effectiveness of Each of Sixteen Sentencing Policies on the
One Hundred Twenty-Six Violent Juvenile Offenders

| | | | Counts Prevented (N = 2622) | | | |
| | Juveniles Prevented | | Arrest Level | | Conviction Level | |
Sentencing Policy	Number	Percent	Number	Percent	Number	Percent
1	28	22.2	30	1.1	23	0.9
2	12	9.5	12	0.5	11	0.4
3	6	4.8	6	0.2	5	0.2
4	33	26.2	35	1.3	27	1.0
5	14	11.1	14	0.5	13	0.5
6	6	4.8	6	0.2	5	0.2
7	9	7.1	9	0.3	8	0.3
8	7	5.6	7	0.3	7	0.3
9	4	3.2	4	0.2	4	0.2
10	11	8.7	11	0.4	10	0.4
11	8	6.3	8	0.3	8	0.3
12	4	3.2	4	0.2	4	0.2
13[a]	−	−	−	−	−	−
14	1	0.8	1	−	1	−
15	1	0.8	1	−	1	−
16[a]	−	−	−	−	−	−
17	1	0.8	1	−	1	−
18	1	0.8	1	−	1	−

[a]Sentencing policies 13 and 16 are logically impossible.

1.3 percent of the total number of violent crimes known to the Columbus police would have been prevented by the previous adoption of a strategy of juvenile incapacitation. The convictions in court that would have been prevented because no crime would have been committed would be just one percent of all the reported crimes of violence. Note also that Policy 1, calling for a three-year sentence for any felony arrest, would have served nearly as well; most of the serious delinquent careers that we are considering are no more than three years long. Table 4-10 provides details of the results of all the options, even though some, as will be seen, are capable of reaching only one individual out of the entire cohort.

Aggregating the Results of Incapacitation

We have now incapacitated everyone who could be incapacitated by sentences imposed by the courts after conviction of an offense. There were 468 individuals who are known to have committed violent offenses in Columbus in 1973; 342 adults, 126 juveniles. We have taken into account their records as offenders during the preceding five years, and have applied various sentencing policies to their felony offenses, if any. Table 4-11 shows the results. Policy 4, five years for any felony, would have prevented 126 persons, men, women and children, from committing 210 offenses for which arrests were made and 105 offenses which were carried through the courts to a 1973 felony conviction. If 26.9 percent of the violent offenders would have been prevented from committing whatever offense was charged against them in 1973, it is to be borne in mind that even at this stringent level, 73.1 percent of those who committed violent offenses could not have been reached by the law. The more realistic options, allowing for three-year sentences would not have reached nearly so many, nor prevented more than a fraction of the known volume of violent crime.

In summarizing these results, the effectiveness of each of the sixteen policies was found to be greater for robbery than for prevention of any other types of violent crimes. More robbers, armed and unarmed, would have been prevented from committing their 1973 violent acts than of violent sex offenders, assault-ists, or murderers. If there is a case to be made, for incapacitation, as a goal for the criminal justice system then the strongest case can be made for robbery. The reason is simple: More of the robbers than of the other groups of violent offenders had a prior felony arrest in the preceding five years, and since a felony arrest between 1968 and 1973 was a prerequisite for an incapacitating sentence, the robbers would most likely have been caught in the net.

Activating any of the policies we have considered would have resulted in protracted terms in confinement for men and women who would not have committed any crime at all during the period for which they would have been incapacitated. It is not entirely impossible to arrive at a justification for such a

Table 4-11
The Effectiveness of Each of the Sixteen Sentencing Policies
on the 468 Franklin County Arrestees in 1973

| | | | Counts Prevented | | | |
| | Persons Prevented | | Arrest Level | | Conviction Level | |
Sentencing Policy	Number	Percent	Number	Percent	Number	Percent
1	78	16.7	116	4.0	59	2.0
2	47	10.0	76	2.6	36	1.2
3	33	7.1	56	1.9	26	0.9
4	126	26.9	210	7.3	105	3.6
5	77	16.5	135	4.7	62	2.1
6	48	10.3	77	2.7	35	1.2
7	26	5.6	33	1.1	23	0.8
8	21	4.5	27	0.9	18	0.6
9	18	3.8	24	0.8	15	0.5
10	49	10.5	78	2.7	49	1.7
11	38	8.1	57	2.0	35	1.2
12	28	6.0	37	1.3	21	0.7
13[a]	–	–	–	–	–	–
14	9	1.9	14	0.5	7	0.2
15	9	1.9	14	0.5	7	0.2
16[a]	–	–	–	–	–	–
17	11	2.4	18	0.6	9	0.3
18	10	2.1	15	0.5	8	0.3

[a]Sentencing Policies 13 and 16 are logically impossible.

harsh policy, if we can assume that the prevention of crime is a transcendent goal that overrides in importance every other consideration. We have not been able to arrive at a cost estimate for each of the sentencing policies in this study. But in 1972, there were about 1,800 adults arrested for felonies in Franklin County alone. If each arrest had led to a conviction and a five-year prison sentence, Franklin County alone would have committed about 9,000 people to the Ohio prison population over a five-year period—about two-thirds the number of men, women, and children now confined in the hard-pressed and crowded incarcerative facilities of the state.

Notes

1. New York State Senate Bill 5A, and Assembly Bill 43, enacted July 14, 1978, effective September 1, 1978. "To provide for a major violent-offense trial program."

2. *Uniform Crime Reports, 1973*, table 75, p. 223.

5

Incapacitation Policies and the False-Positives

Assuming its effectiveness, an assumption which is certainly not supported by our data, what strains would an incapacitation policy impose on the criminal justice system? There are several important issues to explore, two of which call for special attention. The first issue is that of the "false-positives," those felons who would be incapacitated even though, in fact, they would have committed no crime. Our study design is fitted to investigate this question, and in this chapter we shall report our findings about the numbers of Franklin County offenders who would have been needlessly incapacitated had our hypothetical sentencing policies been in effect.

The second issue concerns not the human but the economic costs of incapacitation. After five years under Sentencing Policy 4, Franklin County alone would have committed about two-thirds as many adults to Ohio prisons as are presently in the system. If juveniles were included in the policy, the proportion would be even higher; in contrast, Franklin County includes only 7.8 percent of the population of the state.[1] The most implacable anticrime crusade could hardly expect to include an incapacitation proposal of this magnitude, and we have seen that less sweeping sentencing policies would not be worth the trouble.

To explore the first of these issues, we created a data base consisting of all adults arrested for the commission of a violent felony in 1966 in Franklin County. To do this, we examined every case recorded in the office of the County Clerk of Courts. There were 178 such individuals. With the cooperation of the Columbus Police Department and several other criminal justice agencies in the area, we identified 164 members of this group and then obtained their criminal history from either the FBI or the Ohio Bureau of Criminal Investigation. These criminal histories were current for each individual in this study group through March 1977. All available background information was collected for as thorough a study of this group as we could make under the circumstances.

The 164 members of this study group were similar in sociodemographic characteristics to our 1973 adult felony offenders. The seven stormy years that intervened between 1966 and 1973 failed to alter the street crime arrest trends. The cohort of 164 consisted of 156 males and ninety blacks, (see tables 5-1 and 5-2), and just as with our other cohorts, over 90 percent came from the poorer census tracts, as measured by median income. (See table 5-3.) As to age distribution, the group is a little older than those arrested in 1973, perhaps

Table 5-1
Sex Composition of Cohort

Sex	Number	Percent
Male	156	95.1
Female	8	4.9
Total	164	100.0

because the baby boom of the late 1940s and early 1950s had not yet produced the volume of young adults that was later available. (See table 5-4.)

Criminal Histories

Considering their adult records only, our cohort consisted of sixty-four "virgins," for whom the 1966 arrest was the first on record, seventy-eight recidivists, for whom it was the second, third, or fourth, and twenty-two chronic offenders, with five to sixteen felony arrests. Two-fifths were officially clean up to 1966, 48 percent were multiple violators, and 13 percent were chronic recidivists. (See table 5-5.)

Table 5-6 shows the distribution of crimes for which our 164 offenders were arrested. It is to be remembered that these are police charges, not necessarily the offenses of which these individuals were convicted. On table 5-7, we find the distribution of the cohort by the number of counts preferred against each. Thirty-seven were charged with more than one felony; in one case nine charges were preferred. One of the most interesting elements of our recapitulation shows the length of time required for processing these cases to conclusion. Forty-four of those arrested had the charges dismissed, usually by a motion of *nolle prosequi*. For twenty-one, processing to a conviction took three or fewer months; another thirty-one were out of the way in six months; forty more were concluded within the year. But fourteen were unresolved for more than a year, and one pended for twenty-seven months. (See table 5-8.)

The outcome of prosecution is displayed in table 5-9. Although everyone in

Table 5-2
Racial Composition of Cohort

Race	Number	Percent
Black	90	54.9
White	74	45.1
Total	164	100.0

Table 5-3
Residence Tract Median Income

Median Income	Number	Percent
Below $5,291	30	18.3
$5,292 to $8,465	74	45.1
$8,466 to $10,582	39	23.8
Above $10,582	15	9.1
Not known	6	3.7
Total	164	100.0

the cohort had been arrested on charges of great seriousness, the dispositions tended to reduce the gravity of the charges. In forty-four cases, the charges were dropped entirely, and fourteen more were convicted of misdemeanors. In three cases proceedings were waived by the prosecutor when the defendant was returned to prison as a technical parole violator. Of the 164, 103 were convicted of a felony, a 62.8 percent rate. Sixteen of those subjects were convicted of a second count and four were convicted on three. Note that the number of counts was significantly fewer than the number of original charges. (Compare to table 5-7.) Overall, only 56.7 percent of the 164, ninety-three persons, were convicted of a violent felony.

As all those arrested were charged with violent crimes, a review of the dispositions provides an insight into the need for incapacitation as seen by the county prosecutor and the courts. As we have already noted, charges against forty-four of the cohort were dropped, and fourteen others were reduced to misdemeanors. That reduced the size of the study group by 35 percent, in the sense that no serious effort was made to incapacitate these individuals. The moderate restraint of a term of probation, sometimes fairly long, was imposed on thirty-six individuals, and fourteen were fined and reprimanded from the bench.

The remainder, sixty-nine individuals, were incapacitated by commitments

Table 5-4
Age Composition of Cohort

Age	Number	Percent
Under 21	36	22.0
21-25	38	23.2
26-30	30	18.3
31-40	34	20.7
41-50	14	8.5
51-68	12	7.3
Total	164	100.0

Table 5-5
Number of Felony Arrests Prior to 1966

Prior Felony Arrests	Number	Percent
0	64	39.0
1	46	28.0
2	17	10.4
3	15	9.2
4	5	3.1
5	5	3.1
6	2	1.2
8	3	1.8
9	2	1.2
10	1	0.6
11	1	0.6
12	2	1.2
15	1	0.6
Total	164	100.0

to prison. Some were sentenced to less than a year; four are still serving time in 1978. Distribution of the sentences is shown in table 5-10. It is impressive that only 42 percent of all those arrested for violent offenses in 1966—out of 1,390 reported violent offenses—appeared to the court to require the incapacitating restraint of a commitment to prison.

The 164 subjects arrested and charged with a serious violent crime in 1966 were, like the 468 others described in our two preceding chapters, jacks of many

Table 5-6
Most Serious Crime Charged in 1966 Event

Most Serious Crime	Number	Percent
Murder I	8	4.9
Murder II	5	3.1
Armed robbery	32	14.5
Rape	18	11.0
Unarmed robbery	34	20.7
Carnal knowledge of female under 16	1	0.6
Manslaughter I	4	2.4
Intentional shooting	4	2.4
Sodomy	7	4.2
Assault with intent to rape	2	1.2
Assault with intent to rob	4	2.4
Felonious assault (assault on a minor)	15	9.2
Assault with deadly weapon	26	15.9
Armed robbery of financial institution	3	1.8
Carnal knowledge of an insane female	1	0.6
Total	164	99.9[a]

[a]Error due to rounding.

Table 5-7
Total Felony Charges at Trial

Number of Felonies	Frequency	Percent
1	127	77.5
2	23	14.0
3	9	5.5
4	2	1.2
5	2	1.2
9 or more	1	0.6
Total	164	100.0

criminal trades. We tracked the histories of these 164 cases before, during, and after their index event in 1966. Considering only the single most serious charge per arrest, the 164 subjects had been charged with 637 offenses during the course of their recorded careers. The earliest arrest incident occurred in 1926; the last in 1977. There were forty-eight events logged before 1950; 128 in the 1950s; 102 from 1960 through 1965; 175 in the index year; and 184 after 1966. These 637 offenses, counting only the most serious charge for each arrest, were distributed as shown in table 5-11.

Table 5-12 outlines information on the processing time for the cases completed to a guilty verdict during the careers of the 164 subjects. Two-fifths of the cases were processed in three or fewer months. Another fifth was finished in four to six months. The median processing time was four months, the mode one month, and the average was five months (after disregarding one outlier). One case was diverted to the mental health system and finally closed with a guilty verdict eighty-eight months later. Except for this case, the longest processing time was twenty-seven months. There were 272 cases compiled by the 164 subjects which did not result in known guilty convictions. In 172 of these, the case was dropped or the subject was found not guilty. Five of the cases were still in court in 1977 when the records were gathered. Four cases were sent to the

Table 5-8
Length of Processing Time from Arrest to Case Conclusion

Processing Time	Frequency	Percent
1-3 months	21	12.8
4-6 months	31	18.9
7-12 months	40	24.4
1-2 years	14	8.6
More than 2 years	1	0.6
Length of time unknown	13	7.9
Case dropped	44	26.8
Total	164	100.0

Table 5-9
Charges and Convictions for 1966 Crime

Offense	Number Charged	Number Convicted
Murder I	8	2
Murder II	5	1
Armed robbery	32	20
Rape	18	4
Unarmed robbery	34	24
Carnal knowledge of female under 16	1	2
Manslaughter I	4	10
Intentional shooting	4	4
Sodomy	7	3
Assault to rape	2	2
Assault to rob	4	3
Felonious assault (assault on a minor)	15	10
Assault with deadly weapon	26	6
Armed robbery of financial institution	3	2
Carnal knowledge of an insane female	1	0
Burglary/night season	–	1
Malicious entry	–	1
Auto theft	–	1
Felony larceny	–	3
Pocket picking	–	1
Forgery	–	2
Illegal possession of narcotics	–	1
Parole violator	–	3
Misdemeanor	–	14
Charges dropped/no convictions	–	44

mental health system and closed. For ninety-one of the cases, the disposition was unknown.

With regard to the most serious conviction, it is clear that there was considerable disparity between charge and most serious conviction count. The

Table 5-10
Length of Incarceration of Those Sentenced to Prison for 1966 Crime

Length of Incarceration	Number	Percent
Less than 1 year	5	3.0
1-2 years	5	3.0
2-3 years	11	6.7
3-4 years	10	6.1
4-5 years	9	5.5
5-9 years	17	10.4
Still in prison	4	2.4
Unknown	8	4.9
No incarceration	95	58.0
Total	164	100.0

Table 5-11
Most Serious Charge in Each Arrest During Career of
1966 Cohort

Most Serious Charge	Number	Percent
Murder I	8	1.3
Murder II	7	1.1
Armed robbery	71	11.1
Maiming	1	0.2
Rape	41	6.4
Unarmed robbery	74	11.6
Carnal knowledge of female under 16	3	0.5
Manslaughter I	6	0.9
Intentional shooting	7	1.1
Sodomy	9	1.4
Assault to kill	2	0.3
Assault to rape	3	0.5
Assault to rob	5	0.8
Felonious assault	26	4.1
Assault with deadly weapon	40	6.3
Armed robbery of financial institution	4	0.6
Gross sexual imposition	2	0.3
Carnal knowledge of an insane female	1	0.2
Burglary night season	63	9.9
Breaking and entering (day)	14	2.2
Breaking and entering (night)	9	1.4
Forced entry to coin device	1	0.2
Forced entry	1	0.2
Receive and conceal	5	0.8
Breaking and entering safety deposit	5	0.8
Pocket picking	2	0.3
Auto theft	27	4.2
Operating motor vehicle without owner's consent	5	0.8
Dyer Act	6	0.9
Carrying a concealed weapon	17	2.7
Possession of firearm by felon	4	0.6
Grand larceny	78	12.2
Theft over $100	1	0.2
Larceny by trick	2	0.3
Forgery	28	4.4
Forgery of sales slips	2	0.3
Defrauding innkeeper	1	0.2
Nonsufficient funds	6	0.8
Uttering and publishing forged checks	10	1.6
Fraud	1	0.2
Illegal possession of narcotics	29	4.6
Possession of narcotics for sale	2	0.3
Arson	2	0.3
Embezzlement	1	0.2
Nonsupport	1	0.2
False pretense	1	0.2
Kidnapping	1	0.2
Mail fraud	1	0.2
Counterfeiting	1	0.2
Total[a]	637	100.3

[a]Error due to rounding.

Table 5-12
Length of Processing Time for Cases Completed in Conviction during Career of 1966 Subjects

Processing Time	Number	Percent
1-3 months	149	40.8
4-6 months	73	20.0
7-12 months	63	17.3
13-24 months	22	6.0
Over 24 months	3	0.8
Unknown	55	15.1
Total[a]	365	100.0

[a]Of the remaining 272 cases, 172 were dropped, five are still in court, four resulted into a transfer to the mental health system without trial, and the disposition of ninety-one other cases was unknown.

charges and convictions are set side-by-side in table 5-13 to emphasize this discrepancy. Thus, there were fifteen Murder I or II charges but only two each of these resulted in a finding of guilty to these charges. The seventy-one armed robberies were reduced to thirty-six convictions; the seventy-four unarmed robberies to forty; the forty rape charges resulted in eight convictions. The more serious the charge the more likely a proportionately small conviction count. In contrast, there were six bookings on Manslaughter I but eleven convictions, an increase which can only be explained as the consequence of reduced Murder I or Murder II counts. (See table 5-14.))

Measuring the False-Positives

To incapacitate a criminal is to predict that if he is not confined, he will commit another crime. Such a prediction can be made individually: This man to be sentenced is likely to repeat his offense if he is not incarcerated, and the probability is too great to allow his release. Such predictions are inevitably to be made by those who administer justice, and the responsibility for making them is one of the most ancient duties of the judge. It is not to be expected that society will relieve him of this burden, nor do we argue that it should.

What is under analysis here is the prediction made for all members of a class of criminals. Instead of considering the prospects for an individual in all the factors, objective and subjective, that a court can assemble, the individual criminal is assigned to a class by a characteristic—the commission of a felony, the record of several previous crimes of some specific kind. It is argued by those who believe such a policy should be put into effect that an incapacitating sentence applied to all members of a class will significantly reduce the incidence of crimes

Table 5-13
Most Serious Crime Convictions in Careers of 1966 Cohort

Most Serious Crime Conviction	Number	Percent
Murder I	2	0.3
Murder II	2	0.3
Armed robbery	36	5.7
Rape	8	1.3
Unarmed robbery	40	6.3
Carnal knowledge of female under 16	3	0.5
Manslaughter I	11	1.8
Intentional shooting	5	0.8
Sodomy	3	0.5
Assault to rape	3	0.5
Assault to rob	4	0.6
Felonious assault	13	2.0
Assault with a deadly weapon	8	1.3
Armed robbery of financial institution	3	0.5
Gross sexual imposition	2	0.3
Burglary/night season	17	2.7
Breaking and entering (day)	11	1.8
Malicious entry	3	0.5
Breaking and entering (night)	8	1.3
Receive and conceal	3	0.5
Breaking and entering safety deposit	1	0.2
Auto theft	7	1.1
Operating motor vehicle without owner's consent	3	0.5
Dyer Act	6	0.9
Carry a concealed weapon	3	0.5
Larceny from person	1	0.2
Unlawful claim of money order	1	0.2
Grand larceny	19	3.0
Pocket picking	1	0.2
Forgery	16	2.5
Forgery of sales slips	3	0.5
Defrauding innkeeper	1	0.2
Nonsufficient funds	2	0.3
Uttering and publishing forged checks	3	0.5
Fraud	1	0.2
Illegal possession of narcotics	12	1.9
Possession of narcotics for sale	1	0.2
Nonsupport	1	0.2
False pretense	1	0.2
Mail fraud	1	0.2
Counterfeiting	1	0.2
Case in court	5	0.8
Disposition unknown	91	14.3
Probation or parole violator	18	2.8
Misdemeanor conviction	75	11.8
Case dropped	176	27.6
Total[a]	637	101.0[a]

[a]Error due to rounding.

Table 5-14

A Comparison of the Most Serious Charges and Convictions

Charge	Number of Charges	Number of Convictions
Murder I	8	2
Murder II	7	2
Armed robbery	71	36
Maiming	1	0
Rape	41	8
Unarmed robbery	74	40
Carnal knowledge of female under 16	3	3
Manslaughter I	6	11
Intentional shooting	7	5
Sodomy	9	3
Assault to kill	2	0
Assault to rape	3	3
Assault to rob	5	4
Felonious assault	26	13
Assault with a deadly weapon	40	8
Armed robbery of financial institution	4	3
Gross sexual imposition	2	2
Carnal knowledge of an insane female	1	0
Burglary/night season	63	17
Breaking and entering (day)	14	11
Malicious entry	0	3
Breaking and entering (night)	9	8
Forced entry to coin device	1	0
Forced entry	1	0
Receive and conceal	5	3
Breaking and entering safety deposit	5	1
Pocket picking	2	3
Auto theft	27	7
Operating motor vehicle without owner's consent	5	3
Dyer act	6	6
Carrying a concealed weapon	17	3
Possession of firearm by felon	4	0
Larceny from person	0	1
Unlawful claim of money order	0	1
Grand larceny	78	19
Theft over $100	1	0
Larceny by trick	2	0
Forgery	28	16
Forgery of sales slips	2	3
Defrauding innkeeper	1	1
Nonsufficient funds	6	2
Uttering and publishing forged checks	10	3
Fraud	1	1
Illegal possession of narcotics	29	12
Possession of narcotics for sale	2	1
Arson	2	0
Embezzlement	1	0
Nonsupport	1	1
False pretense	1	1
Kidnapping	1	0
Mail fraud	1	1

Table 5-14 continued

Charge	Number of Charges	Number of Convictions
Counterfeiting	1	1
Case in court	0	5
Disposition unknown	0	91
Probation or parole violator	0	18
Misdemeanor conviction	0	75
Case dropped	0	176
Total	637	637

that society want to diminish. In previous chapters we have shown that the reduction of violent crime to be expected from such a policy will not be great, even assuming an impractically harsh sentencing policy.

Here we shall measure the human cost inevitable in the application of a blunderbuss approach to the administration of criminal justice. It is in the nature of prediction that some will be wrong. When they are made in mass, their usefulness depends on the frequency of error. If the human phenomena to be predicted are fairly well understood, the incorrect predictions may be tolerated, as for example in the case of predicting success in school, consumer response to a new commercial product, or effective play on a football team. In the case of incapacitating criminals, the cost is great in both human and economic dimensions and the elements of a prediction formula are not well understood. Wasted years in prison are heavy costs for the offender who is needlessly incarcerated. Public funds allocated to unnecessary man-years will rise. It becomes a matter of responsible policy formulation to measure the extent to which incapacitating policies will restrain people who would not in fact commit a crime for which restraint is needed.

To make such a measurement, we again undertook to find out what would have happened if a blanket sentencing policy had been applied to our 1966 cohort instead of the individualized decision-making that actually happened. We have already seen that the processing that took place was so unpredictable and so erratic that it could not be said that there was any intention at all of reducing criminal behavior by incapacitating all violent offenders for some specific period of time. We asked our data base what would have happened if our sentencing policy 10—five years in prison for the conviction of any violent offense—had been applied to this cohort. Obviously, sentencing policy 4, which was the principal vehicle for the study of the effectiveness of incapacitation, would not apply to this cohort, composed as it is of persons arrested for violent felonies.

Our strategy for this calculation was simple. Since the incapacitation policy we tested would lock up convicted felons for five years on the assumption that many crimes would thereby be prevented, we thought that an appropriate measure of true-positives would be to measure criminal activity during the first five years of freedom after conviction. Our unit of measurement was a felony arrest or conviction, or, as a subset, a violent felony arrest or conviction. If there were a period of incarceration after the 1966 conviction, the period for measurement would be the first five years after release. There were a few cases in which the prisoner was released after 1972, and thus with less than five full years before the end of the study interval in 1977; they were not considered in this part of the study. Data were lacking on the length of confinement of eight prisoners; we assigned them the median length of incarceration, forty-one months.

Our calculation took in all those who recidivated during five years of freedom and compared that total to the eligible number of offenders in the 1966 study group. Three groups were used as denominators for the study: (1) all persons arrested in 1966 for a violent felony, 164; (2) all persons convicted of a felony in 1966 as a consequence of an arrest for a violent incident, 103, who returned to the street in time for at least four years of freedom, 98; and (3) all persons convicted of a violent felony as a consequence of their arrest on a charge of a violent offense in 1966, 93, and returned to the street in time for at least four years of freedom, 88. Ten persons arrested for violent crimes were convicted of nonviolent offenses. Only three offenders were squeezed into the eligible population by requiring only four years of freedom instead of the five to be matched against sentencing policy 10.

Table 3-38 shows the reduction in violent crime that would result from the application of sentencing policy 10 to adult offenders. Of the entire cohort of 342 offenders in 1973, only 5.8 percent would have been prevented from committing their offense in 1973; counting the arrests of the 342 against 2,892 crimes of violence, only 1.3 percent of that total would have been prevented. Counting the convictions against the total number of crimes reported, 0.8 percent of the total would have been prevented. We must weigh this level of crime reduction against the number of false-positives to be locked up as a result of rigorous application of sentencing policy 10.

There are several approaches to the determination of the division of our study group into true and false positives. Figure 5-1 illustrates the calculations. It will be seen that of the 164 persons arrested and charged, 103 (62.8 percent) were convicted of a felony, and ninety-three (56.7 percent) of these convictions were for a crime of violence.

Of the 103 convictions, ninety-eight were released with sufficient time for us to study their careers for inclusion in this analysis. Thirty-nine of these individuals were rearrested on felony charges during the five years after release, of whom twenty-nine were ultimately convicted of a felony offense. Only nine of these convictions were violent. Thus sentencing policy 10 would have resulted in the prevention of the crimes committed by 17.7 percent of the whole cohort (164 persons), at the expense of 82.3 percent of the cohort who were not convicted at all. These would have been individuals confined for five years for the purpose of incapacitation who, in fact, were convicted of no crime, violent or nonviolent.

The analysis of the chain of events from first conviction to a reconviction of a new violent crime is even more impressive. Ninety-three individuals had been convicted of violent crimes (ten were convicted of nonviolent offenses and are disregarded at this point). Of this number, four were never released, one was released too late to accumulate experience for this study, and eighty-eight were available for analysis. Only eighteen of these eighty-eight were rearrested on charges of a violent offense and only nine reconvicted. The true-positives, persons who would have been prevented from committing a crime of violence if a five-year sentence had been imposed at the time of the first conviction, were 20.5 and 10.2 percent, using an arrest or conviction assumption, respectively. The remaining proportion would have been needlessly imprisoned if the intent of such a sentence was solely to incapacitate.

The inescapable conclusions of this phase of our research are these:

1. The police clear a small proportion of the violent crimes reported to them. While there are differences, the over-all arrest rate for violent crimes is between 22 and 30 percent, a rate which had not changed significantly for years, even with increased resources and some improvements in technology.

2. An arrest for violence does not assure a conviction for a violent crime. The attrition is about 40 percent of those arrested.

3. Conviction does not necessarily result in a prison term; only sixty-nine of the original 164 persons arrested were imprisoned, or 67.0 percent of the 103 actual felony convictions.

4. About two-thirds of those incarcerated served terms of less than five years.

Implications

This experiment demonstrates that the strategy of incapacitation of violent offenders fails to reduce street crimes of violence by a significant margin, and, if applied as recommended by some commentators, would result in enormous human and economic costs far out of proportion to the volume of crime prevented. Of our original 164 persons arrested, ninety-three were convicted of a violent felony, eighty-eight were released, and only nine were reconvicted of another violent crime. That results in a 90 percent margin of error, far too wide to justify by the standards of justice as traditionally administered in this country.

It may be argued that we have over-stated the consequences of incapacitation. Three points might be made against us:

1. People who have been convicted of heinous offenses deserve no sympathy. If all such persons cannot be apprehended, at least society can announce

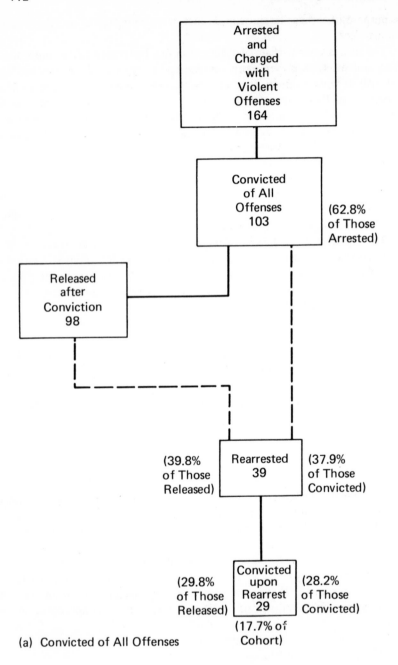

(a) Convicted of All Offenses

Figure 5-1. Flow Chart of Successive Dispositions of 164 Violent Offenders Arrested i 1966: (a) Convicted of All Offenses (b) Convicted of Violent Offenses.

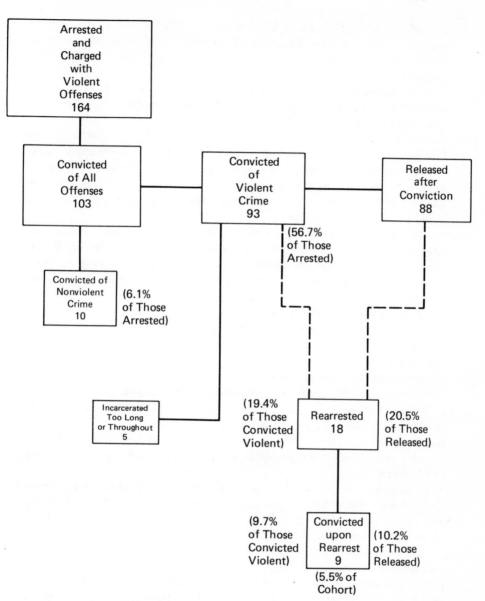

(b) Convicted of Violent Offenses

through the courts that certain kinds of offenses will not be tolerated. No one can know which of these dangerous offenders will erupt into violence again; those who commit such crimes must be treated as violent whatever their probable future may be.

This argument is beside the point. Violent crimes cannot be prevented in sufficient numbers to reduce the rate of violent crime more than marginally, and that marginal reduction must be at enormous cost.

2. No one knows how many offenses the 90 percent of our cohort who were false-positives really committed after their release. Surely, many among these seventy-nine offenders were false-positives only because the police could not catch and convict them. If we do not know for sure, an incapacitation strategy assures that the undetected crimes which the false-positives may have committed would not in fact be committed.

This argument presupposes a willingness to change the fundamental assumptions of the law, and, in principle, can neither be refuted nor confirmed. What is certain, however, is that the implementation of any of our sentencing policies would result in huge economic costs whether or not the human costs can be accepted in our society.

3. Some may argue that the breakdown of nine true- and seventy-nine false-positives is a misrepresentation. They will note that on table 5-3 about 37 percent of the original 164 subjects were over thirty-one years old at the time of the 1966 arrest. Some may have died, or been disabled, or have come to the natural end of their criminal careers. It is not unreasonable to guess that no more than forty-four of the eighty-eight subjects could have reasonably been expected to be true positives. If so, the nine actual violent offenders represent 20 percent of the total number of persons likely to be true-positives. Counting in the additional offenses for which the true-positives were not apprehended but probably committed, it is conceivable that the number of true-positives is close to 50 percent.

The answer to this argument is obvious: All eighty-eight would have been incapacitated under the application of sentencing policy 10. If half the eighty-eight were unlikely to commit another crime of violence, the unfairness of the policy is even more grievous.

Apologists for the hard line refuse to be squeamish about the plight of persons who are treated as dangerous even though they are not. We hold that punishment must be based on conviction after a day in court. If a crime is serious enough to require a long prison term as retribution, the offender is incapacitated as a by-product of appropriate punishment. If it is not sufficiently serious for such a term of punishment, to administer it anyway leads to a transformation of long-established principles of justice which still serve to protect the liberty of the citizen.

Note

1. *U.S. Census of Population: 1970–United States Summary*, page 1-48, table 8, and page 1-104, table 24.

6

The Limits of Prevention

Overview of the Research and Its Conclusions

This research was designed to measure the effectiveness of incapacitation as a strategy for the prevention of violent crime. To begin with, we list our conclusions; we will then outline their implications for the making of policy in the administration of criminal justice.

1. Application of our most severe sentencing policy, which provides for a flat five-year term for any adult or juvenile convicted of a felony, would have prevented the 210 violent crimes for which arrests were made in 1973, or 7.3 percent of the 2,892 such crimes reported. But the number of crimes for which a conviction was obtained constituted 3.6 percent of the total.

2. Assuming that recidivists commit the same proportion of uncleared crimes as they commit of those cleared by the police, it is possible that 26.7 percent of the reported crimes of violence might have been prevented.

3. If it is assumed that recidivists committed a larger percentage of the uncleared crimes than they did of the cleared crimes, the number of crimes prevented would exceed 26.7 percent.

4. If the uncleared crimes are attributed to first offenders—whether arrested or not—the value of incapacitation may fall considerably below the 26.7 percent.

5. The most reasonable and probable effect of the sentencing policy 4 is a prevention level falling between 7.3 and 26.7 percent. Our opinion is that this level must be less than the upper limit because recidivists are more liable to arrest—being previously known to the police—than are virgins in crime.

6. A more reasonable sentencing policy, five years incarceration on a second felony conviction, to be imposed on both juveniles and adults, will yield prevention values of 4.7 percent at the level of arrest, (compared to 7.3 percent for sentencing policy 4) and 2.1 percent at the conviction level. If these values are extrapolated to account for the uncleared crimes, the prevention value will rise to about 17 percent.

7. If incapacitating sentences are reserved for violent offenders only, as in sentencing policy 10, five years for any violent felony, whether committed by adult or juvenile offenders, the number of violent offenses prevented in 1973 would constitute 2.7 percent at the level of arrest, and 1.7 percent at the level of conviction. The extrapolation for uncleared offenses would yield a prevention value of 9.8 percent.

8. There is substantial variability in the prevention potential by category of

offense. Returning to the application of sentencing policy 4, (five years flat for any felony) whereby 26.7 percent of the reported cleared felonies would have been prevented, we find that 34.4 percent of the murders, 29.9 percent of the robberies, 25.5 percent of the forcible sex offenses, and only 12.9 percent of the aggravated assaults would have been prevented. In real numbers, these percentages are translated into twenty-two of the sixty-four homicides, 130 of the 435 robberies, forty-one of the 161 sex offenses, and seventeen of the 132 felonious assaults. Counting offenders rather than offenses, twenty-two of the fifty-one murderers, ninety of the 258 robbers, twenty-six of the 112 sex offenders, and fourteen of the 100 assaultists would have been prevented from committing the acts with which they were charged in 1973.

9. To accomplish the goals of sentencing policy 4 would result in the increase of commitments from Franklin County by about 500-600 percent. For the whole state of Ohio the result would be an increase in prison population, after five years of this policy in force, of from about 13,000 to at least 65,000.

10. We collected data to establish the percentage of those who would have been confined under a policy of sentencing violent offenders to five years in prison but who in fact did not commit a subsequent violent crime. Of the universe of 164 adults arrested for a crime of violence in 1966, ninety-three were convicted, eighty-eight were returned to the community and nine were reconvicted within five years of street time of a violent crime. This yields a percentage of false-positives amounting to 90 percent, an intolerable margin of error.

In the remainder of this chapter we will present the connections between our data, as shown in the earlier chapters of this book, and the findings outlined above.

Boundaries for Speculation

Until this chapter we have practiced self-denial. We have stuck to our data and avoided speculation. We have shown where the data will take us when we apply various sentencing policies designed for the exclusive purpose of incapacitation, without any consideration of the other aims of criminal justice. Our question has been subjunctive: What would have happened to the incidence of violent crime in Columbus if certain policies had been faithfully applied by the courts to certain real offenders, instead of the sentences actually imposed on them? To our knowledge, this study is the first empirical approach designed exclusively to address the question of incapacitation; from the start we intended to assess the potential and costs of incapacitation and our data were gathered only to that end.

Our answers have settled on the minimum levels of crime reduction that might be affected by incarcerating these offenders. The results show that the reduction of crime would be slight. Even sentencing policy 4, whereby offenders, both adult and juvenile, convicted of *any* felony, violent or nonviolent, would be committed to irreducible terms of five years in prison, would do no more than nibble at the volume of reported violence. The 210 crimes against the person for which arrests were made, as shown above, constituted only 7.3 percent of the 2,892 such crimes reported. But these arrests resulted in only 105 convictions; 3.6 percent of all the violent crimes reported.

That much is a simple factual demonstration. It requires no special insight to perceive that some of the persons arrested in 1973 must have committed more crimes than those for which they were charged. It will be rightly contended that more than 210 crimes might have been prevented by incapacitation.

There were exactly 2,100 of the 2,892 violent crimes reported for which we could find no record of an arrest. Speculation must now supplement the process of counting. We must arrive at an estimate of the number of uncleared offenses that can be allocated to members of our cohort. It is a confusing problem, the solution to which requires us to establish a system of boundaries to the possibilities allowed by the data.

Estimating by Quadrants

To be useful, speculation must be disciplined so far as possible by reality. Assumptions must be made, but they must be limited by the data. To mark off the boundaries, we have separated the realities and the assumptions in a figure of four quadrants. Table 6-1 displays the foundation of this analysis.

An explanation of table 6-1 is in order. All of the 2892 violent crimes which we examined were committed by persons matching one of four descriptions. Quadrant I is composed of individuals previously convicted of a felony (within three or five years, depending on the policy being considered) and arrested in 1973 for a violent felony. Quadrant II represents those arrested in 1973 for a violent felony, as in quadrant I, but without the recent felony conviction through which the 1973 offense might have been prevented. In contrast, quadrants III and IV represent the crimes of those committing a violent offense

Table 6-1
Quadrant Definition

	1968 to 1973	
1973	*Felony Conviction*	*No Felony Conviction*
Violent arrest in 1973	I	II
No violent arrest in 1973	III	IV

Note: The offenses committed by subjects in Quadrants I and III are theoretically preventable under sentencing policy 4. Those in Quadrants II and IV are not.

during 1973 when the offender was never apprehended for any of those offenses. This group can be subdivided into those recently guilty of a felony conviction—quadrant III—and those who had no such conviction—quadrant IV.

Quadrant I consists of the firm ground of ratified knowledge. We know how many people were arrested for violent crimes in 1973, how many crimes were charged against them, and how many of these offenders had felony convictions within the previous five years. So that all our sentencing policies could be tested, we also know how many convictions these offenders had on their records.

Quadrant II also contains ratified data. We know how many 1973 violent offenders had no recorded felony convictions between 1968 and 1973, and inferences can be drawn from this knowledge, to which we shall return presently.

In quadrant III we can estimate the number of felony convictions during the period 1968-1973 in Franklin County. We have counted the total for one year—1091 felony convictions of all kinds in 1973—and estimated that the total for the whole quinquennium was 5,455, five times the total for 1972. For rough purposes, this rough estimate is all we need. But we do not know how many uncleared violent crimes these people may have committed—obviously they did not commit any crimes that were cleared by the police. It is here that speculation must begin in earnest. It is also in this quadrant that we must consider the number of false-positives, that is, the number of felons convicted during those five years whose incarceration would have been needless because they did not in fact commit a violent crime in 1973.

Finally, in quadrant IV we enter the realm of pure speculation. The only guidance we have on the numbers of crimes to be assigned to this quadrant comes from the estimates of the uncleared crimes assigned to the other three quadrants. The remaining uncleared crimes must have been committed by persons who are not known to the police. They may have been transients passing through town who escaped detection; they may have been residents of Columbus who were never caught. In either case such individuals may have belonged in one of the other three quadrants if we knew who they were, but they may also be persons never known to the police who have succeeded in eluding arrest not only in 1973 but perhaps on other occasions. We do not know and cannot find out how many such persons there may be. To concede their existence is to complete the outline of possibilities.

*Quadrant Distribution for Sentencing
Policy 4*

Table 6-2 shows a distribution of our data which places all the uncleared crimes in quadrants III and IV. It will be seen that under the rules of sentencing policy 4, 210 crimes are placed in quadrant I and 582 go into quadrant II. If we divide

Table 6-2
**Possible Estimate of Prevention of 2,892 Violent Crimes, by Type,
under Sentencing Policy 4, if All Uncleared Crime Committed
by Those not Arrested During 1973**

	Preventable			*Not Preventable*		
	Quadrant I	*Quadrant III*		*Quadrant II*	*Quadrant IV*	
Offense Type	*Cleared*	*Uncleared*	*Total*	*Cleared*	*Uncleared*	*Total*
Murder and nonnegligent manslaughter	22	1	23	42	0	42
Violent sex crimes	41	44	85	120	121	241
Aggravated assault	17	219	236	115	596	711
Robbery	130	301	431	305	818	1123
Total	210	565	775	582	1535	2117

Percent Preventable = 26.7

the uncleared crimes between quadrants III and IV according to the same percentage distribution obtained for the upper two quadrants, we find that 565 are assigned to quadrant III, still uncleared but prevented by sentencing policy 4. But 1,535 would go into quadrant IV—uncleared and unpreventable. If this were the true distribution, 26.7 percent of the 2892 violent felonies of 1973 would have been prevented.

This crude distribution must be wide of the mark. Some of the uncleared offenses must be allocated to quadrants I and II, crimes committed by persons who were arrested either as recidivists or as "virgins" in crime. Table 6-3 shows what our quadrants would look like if we allocated *all* the uncleared offenses to the upper quadrants.

This is an impossible distribution, too. It does, however, reveal the maximum numbers of each category of offense that could be assigned to these quadrants. Turning to the data for each offense category, we find that there was only one uncleared homicide. It will have to be assigned arbitrarily; for the time being, we assign it to quadrant I. There were 165 uncleared violent sex offenses to be distributed between twenty-six recidivists and eighty-six virgins. Allowing forty-four to the former and 121 to the latter, we arrive at a credible but untenable assumption that each such offender committed about one more offense than the one with which he was charged. That could not be true unless none of the individuals in the universes in quadrants III and IV committed a reported sex offense; a most improbable inference. The seventeen recidivists arrested for felonious assaults must be presumed to have committed 219 such offenses for which they were not arrested, and the 115 first offenders are allocated 596 uncleared reports. Even though we have some reason to suppose that assaultists are usually not charged on the first few occasions—as in the case of family fights—it strains credulity to conclude that our seventeen recidivist

Table 6-3
Possible Estimate of Prevention of 2,892 Violent Crimes, by Type, Under Sentencing Policy 4, if Arrested Persons Committed All Crimes

Offense Type	Quadrant I Preventable			Quadrant II Not Preventable		
	Cleared	Uncleared	Total	Cleared	Uncleared	Total
Murder and nonnegligent manslaughter	22	1	23	42	0	42
Violent sex crimes	41	44	85	120	121	241
Aggravated assault	17	219	236	115	596	711
Robbery	130	301	431	305	818	1123
Total	210	565	775	582	1535	2117

Percent Preventable = 26.7

assaultists committed nearly thirteen assaults apiece in 1973 before a victim was willing to sign a warrant for arrest. It seems probable that there are many assaults which were "cleared by investigation" but committed by persons not previously known to the police. Logic puts them in quadrant II; these incidents could not have been prevented, but we have no basis for estimating how many there were.

As to robbery, the ceiling must be lower than some of the estimates thought likely by some commentators. We can assign only 2.8 uncleared robberies per recidivist and 3.3 robberies per virgin. These averages may represent a very wide range. It is not at all inconceivable that some of our robbers may have committed ten or more uncleared robberies, but the more there were of them, the more robbers there must have been who fell the first time out.

This allocation ascribes an infallible efficiency to the Columbus police. It assumes that all the violent offenders caught in this jurisdiction committed all the violent offenses that were committed. That assumption defies belief. Some of the uncleared crimes must be assigned to quadrants III and IV.

Table 6-4 presents the first step toward our best estimate. We assume that each violent sex offender committed one additional sex offense that was not cleared; each assaultist committed four uncleared assaults; each robber committed three uncleared robberies. The percentage of preventable crimes in quadrant I rises to 19.5 percent; those in quadrant II that could not be prevented constitute 52.4 percent of the 2,892 crimes reported.

This allocation to quadrants I and II leaves 813 uncleared crimes to distribute. Some of them must have been committed by persons who had previously been convicted of felonies, but not all of them. If, as shown in table 6-5, we assign them to quadrant III, we discover that 47.6 percent of the 1973 violent felonies are preventable. That is an absurd conclusion, too. It is not reasonable to assume that no crimes were committed by persons unknown to the

Table 6-4
First Step Toward Our Best Estimate of Prevention of 2,892
Violent Crimes by Type, Under Sentencing Policy 4[a]

	Quadrant I Preventable			Quadrant II Not Preventable		
Offense Type	Cleared	Uncleared	Total	Cleared	Uncleared	Total
Murder and nonnegligent manslaughter	22	1	23	42	0	42
Violent sex crimes	41	26	67	120	86	206
Aggravated assault	17	56	73	115	344	459
Robbery	130	270	400	305	504	809
Total	210	353	563	582	934	1516

Percent Preventable = 19.5

[a]Based on assumption that each offender arrested, depending on type of major crime charged, also committed one additional violent sex offense, four other aggravated assaults and three extra robberies in 1973. These add-on crimes did not result in an arrest or charge. Note that 813 crimes are still to be assigned to Quadrants III and IV.

police, especially when we consider that the majority of cleared crimes of violence had to be assigned to quadrant II.

Table 6-6 shows the distribution that would result if we assume that the division between the lower quadrants is the same as we found between the upper two. Adding the 160 uncleared offenses on quadrant III to the 563 we have assigned to quadrant I, we have a total of 723 preventable offenses, exactly 25 percent of all the reported violent offenses.

A final estimate which might be used to set a reasonable upper limit on the effectiveness of sentencing policy 4 would be to assume that twice as large a proportion of the crimes in quadrants III and IV are committed by repeat felons

Table 6-5
Maximum Prevention of 2,892 Violent Crimes, by Type,
in Each Quadrant Under Sentencing Policy 4[a]

Offense Type	I	II	III	IV
Murder and nonnegligent manslaughter	23	42	1	0
Violent sex crimes	67	206	53	0
Aggravated assault	73	459	415	0
Robbery	400	809	344	0
Total	563	1516	813	0

Percent Preventable = 47.6

[a]Based on assumption that no one but arrestees, past or present, committed all 2,892 violent crimes in 1973.

Table 6-6
Probable Distribution of 2,892 Violent Crimes, by Type,
in Each Quadrant Under Sentencing Policy 4[a]

Offense Type	Quadrant			
	I	II	III	IV
Murder and nonnegligent manslaughter	23	42	1	0
Violent sex crimes	67	206	13	40
Aggravated assault	73	459	53	362
Robbery	400	809	93	251
Total	563	1516	160	653

Percent Preventable = 25.0

[a]Based on assumption that uncleared crimes fall into Quadrants III and IV in the same proportions as into Quadrants I and II.

as is true of crimes assigned to quadrants I and II. Since 26.5 percent of the cleared crimes were assigned to quadrant I, we shall assume that quadrant III contains 53.0 percent of the 813 crimes allotted to unapprehended offenders. If this were so, then the total proportion of crimes which might have been prevented through the imposition of a mandatory five-year sentence would be 34.4 percent, 994 of the total 2,892 violent offenses. (See table 6-7.) This, it seems to us, would be the maximum limit, indeed a very generous maximum, of the impact of incapacitation on the crime rate in Franklin County, Ohio, in 1973.

Table 6-7
Reasonable Maximum Distribution of 2,892 Violent Crimes, by Type,
in Each Quadrant Under Sentencing Policy 4[a]

Offense Type	Quadrant			
	I	II	III	IV
Murder and nonnegligent manslaughter	23	42	1	0
Violent sex crimes	67	206	28	25
Aggravated assault	73	459	220	195
Robbery	400	809	182	162
Total	563	1516	431	382

Percent Preventable = 34.4

[a]Based on assumption that uncleared crimes in Quadrants III and IV are twice as frequently committed by repeat felons as was true for known cases in Quadrants I and II.

The Cost of the Hard Line

So far we have made our calculations under the rules of sentencing policy 4. We have already commented that the application of this policy would have unacceptably severe consequences. In quadrant III we can reckon the costs, both economic and social. As noted above, there were 1,091 adult felony convictions in Franklin County during 1972. Of this number, 438 resulted in prison sentences. We could not obtain data that would enable us to calculate an average sentence for those who were incarcerated. For this speculation, we assume a two-year average term. If sentencing policy 4 were put into effect, these 1,091 persons to be incapacitated would impose an additional load on the prison system of 4,629 man-years from Franklin County alone.[1] The increase would be 523 percent.

If over a period of five years Franklin County felons accumulated at the same rate as for 1972, by the end of the fifth year we arrive at an additional population in Ohio prisons of 4,600. If we concede that this figure may be too high by perhaps as much as 40 percent, the state would still have to find room for at least 2,760 additional prisoners from Franklin County. Since the population of Franklin County is one-twelfth that of Ohio and assuming a uniform rate of commitment to the prison system, we arrive at an estimate of about 33,000 prisoners in addition to the approximately 9,000 in custody in 1972. The absurdity of such a result is obvious, even if the reduction in violent crime were much more considerable than the 25-30 percent range so far indicated.[2] Indeed, the reduction would probably be less than that level, since in this instance we are applying policy 4 only in adult courts.

Before we leave this extravagant transformation of the criminal justice system, we must suggest the human costs. Sentencing policy 4 throws into sharp relief the impracticality of incapacitation as the primary objective of the criminal justice system. Disregarding the immense fiscal investment to be allocated to the construction and operation of new penal facilities, the changes in the social structure of the nation that would result from such a policy would be of dimensions that would leave the imagination no base from which to take flight. Over the years, more than the 42,000 felons suggested above would accumulate in Ohio, a state with a population of about 10,000,000. Increasing the incarcerated population by at least four-fold—probably more—would have consequences of greater magnitude, even though they could not readily be translated into statistical projections. A sense of injustice would pervade the whole society—injustice done to and felt by the thousands of young, black, and poor who would compose the preponderance of the distended prison population. Throughout the comfortable classes there would be an inescapable sense of uneasy guilt, not to be offset by the dubious safety afforded by severe repression. If we lower our sights, the reduction in violent crime will be much less significant. Sentencing policy 1 calls for a three-year term upon the conviction of any felony. Applying the same distribution of uncleared crimes that we used with sentencing policy 4, the number of crimes that might be prevented would be in the order of about 11 percent for a policy aimed at adults only. The increase in the prison population at the end of three years would be 2,417, again from Franklin County alone. Again allowing for a state-wide impact of about 12 times the volume of commitment from Franklin County, the increase in population might be about 29,000. If we assume that this figure is as much as 40 percent too high, as we did in estimating the effect of sentencing policy 4, the increase would be 1,450 for Franklin County, and well over 17,000 for the state.

Incapacitation is the strategy of failure; the failure of intimidation and of rehabilitation. As noted it is also a very costly approach to crime reduction. If implemented, it will overwhelm our facilities and incarcerate so many "false-positives" that it will be without much justification or virtue. Its advocates have also overlooked one essential element in this approach. Fundamentally, an incapacitation policy is a prediction policy and an inherently very inefficient one: *The prediction of future violations is based exclusively on prior convictions.* No allowance can be made in the strategy for the extinction of criminal behavior by and through maturation, or by changes in the life situations of prior offenders. Such inflexibility would soon undermine support of this policy; the introduction of flexibility in the form of such additional predictors as age, sex, marital status, and the presence or absence of an alcohol or drug problem would destroy the very invariance which makes incapacitation a seemingly just response to an admittedly insoluble problem.

The results speak for themselves. To incarcerate a specific offender with a record of specific and frequent violent crimes is justified by appealing to the responsibility of the state to protect citizens from probable dangers. A considerable number of predictable crimes may be avoided by individual decisions to incapacitate an offender from committing another offense if permitted to remain at liberty. Not even the most ardent advocate of prison demobilization will dispute the duty of the criminal justice system to make judgments of this kind. Confronted with the evidence that a convicted offender is dangerous, the propriety of his indefinite detention appears obvious to those who would abolish the prison for the punishment of any other kind of criminal. Such predictions may be wrong, and the hazard of the false-positive decision has been assessed in chapter 5 of this book. But a recidivist violent offender with no discernible prospects for change is not difficult to separate from others whose prospects are more favorable and with whom the court is well advised to assume a modest risk of failure.

The distinction to be made lies between individualized judgments and the adoption of categoric strategies which obliterate important differences in favor of the simplicities of statistical prediction. To achieve a modest reduction in the crime rate by assigning individuals to statistical classes will require the creation of an enormous class of persons who are to be designated and treated as potential offenders to be incapacitated at social and economic costs vastly disproportionate to the gain in public safety. To respond to the dictum of James Q. Wilson, it is not true that society knows how to incapacitate. The occasional wicked person to whose wickedness everyone agrees can be incarcerated under maximum restraint, but not because the harm he might do is statistically significant. His restraint is required by our judgment that the handful of victims he might choose must be protected from predictable harm. But we do not know how to bound a whole class of wicked people, and the evidence of this research suggests that we never will.

Notes

1. We arrive at this figure by calculating 3,315 man-years of prison time for the 663 felons who were not incarcerated, and 1,314 additional man-years for 438 who were assumed to have been sentenced to two-year terms.

2. Using a methodology similar to ours, with data drawn from the district court of Denver, Colorado, during the period 1968-1970, Petersilia and Greenwood arrived at results strikingly similar to ours. See Joan Petersilia and Peter W. Greenwood, *Mandatory Prison Sentences: Their Projected Effects on Crime and Prison Population* (Santa Monica, Calif.: Rand Corporation, 1977).

These authors found that a sentencing policy providing for a five-year sentence for *any* felony would have prevented 31 percent of the violent crimes committed during this period, at a cost in increased prison population of 450 percent. A one-year sentence on conviction of any felony yielded a prevention value of 10.9 percent, with an increase in prison population of 25 percent. In general, incapacitation policies were more effective in reducing property crimes than violent offenses.

Bibliography

Avi-Itzhak, Benjamin and Shinnar, Reuel. "Quantitative Models in Crime Control," *Journal of Criminal Justice* 1:185-217, 1973.

Bentham, Jeremy. *Works* (Bowring Edition, reproduced from volumes published in 1838-1843 by Russell and Russell, New York: 1962).

Blumstein, Alfred and Cohen, Jacqueline. "A Theory of the Stability of Punishment," *Journal of Criminal Law and Criminology* 64(2):198-207, Summer, 1973.

Blumstein, Alfred and Nagin, Daniel. "On the Optimum Use of Incarceration for Crime Control," unpublished paper, Urban Systems Institute of the School of Urban and Public Affairs, Carnegie-Mellon University, October, 1976.

Blumstein, Alfred; Cohen, Jacqueline; and Nagin, Daniel (eds.). *Deterrence and Incapacitation: Estimating the Effects of Criminal Sanctions on Crime Roles*, Washington, D.C.: National Academy of Sciences, 1978.

Blumstein, Alfred; Cohen, Jacqueline; and Nagin, Daniel. "The Dynamics of a Homeostatic Punishment Process," *Journal of Criminal Law and Criminology* 67(3):317-334, Fall, 1976.

Boland, Barbara. "Incapacitation of the Dangerous Offender: The Arithmetic Is Not So Simple," *Journal of Research in Crime and Delinquency* 15(1):126-129, January, 1978.

Boland, Barbara. "Punishing Habitual Criminals," *Wall Street Journal* April 11, 1978.

Boland, Barbara and Wilson, James Q. "Age, Crime and Punishment," *The Public Interest* 51:22-34, Spring, 1978.

Clarke, Stevens H. "Getting 'em Out of Circulation: Does Incarceration of Juvenile Offenders Reduce Crime?", *Journal of Criminal Law and Criminology* 65(4):528-535, December, 1974.

Cohen, Jacqueline. "The Incapacitative Effect of Imprisonment: A Critical Review of the Literature," in Alfred Blumstein, Jacqueline Cohen and Daniel Nagin (eds.). *Deterrence and Incapacitation: Estimating the Effects of Criminal Sanctions on Crime Rates.* Washington, D.C.: National Academy of Sciences, 1978.

Collins, James J., Jr. "Chronic Offender Careers," Unpublished paper, Presented at American Society of Criminology Annual Meeting, Nov. 4-7, 1976, Tucson, Arizona.

Conrad, John P. *Crime and Its Correction.* Berkeley: University of California Press, 1965.

Conrad, John and Dinitz, Simon. *In Fear of Each Other.* Lexington, Mass.: Lexington Books, 1977.

Cook, Philip J. "Punishment and Crime: A Critique of Current Findings Concerning the Preventive Effects of Punishment," *Law and Contemporary Problems.* 41:164-204, Winter, 1977.

Criminal Victim Surveys in Cincinnati. National Criminal Justice Information and Statistics Service, SD-NCS-C-9, July 1977.

Criminal Victimization in the United States. National Criminal Justice Information and Statistics Service, SD-NCS-N-7, December 1977.

Curtis, Lynn A. *Criminal Violence.* Lexington, Mass.: Lexington Books, 1974.

Dershowitz, Alan M. "Criminal Sentencing in the United States: An Historical and Conceptual Overview," *Annals of the American Academy of Political and Social Science* 423:117-132, Jan., 1976.

Dershowitz, Alan M. "The Law of Dangerousness: Some Fictions About Predictions," *Journal of Legal Education* 23:25-47, 1970-1971.

Dinitz, Simon and Conrad, John P. "Thinking About Dangerous Offenders," *Criminal Justice Abstracts* 10(1):99-130, March 1978.

Ehrlich, Isaac. "Participation in Illegitimate Activities: An Economic Analysis," *Journal of Political Economy* 81(3):521-567, 1974.

Falkin, Gregory P. "Finding a Cost-Effective Policy to Reduce Juvenile Delinquency," Paper presented at the 25th Annual Meeting of the National Institute on Crime and Delinquency, Miami, Florida, June, 1978.

Foote, Caleb. "Preventive Detention—What Is the Issue?", *The Prison Journal* 50(1):3-11, 1970.

Fogel, David. *We Are The Living Proof.* Cincinnati: W.H. Anderson, 1975.

Gibbs, Jack P. *Crime, Punishment and Deterrence.* New York: Elsevier, 1975.

Gottfredson, Don; Wilkins, Leslie T. and Hoffman, Peter B. *Guidelines for Sentencing and Parole*, Lexington, Mass.: Lexington Books, 1978.

Greenberg, David F. "The Incapacitative Effects of Imprisonment: Some Estimates," *Law and Society Review* 9:541-580, 1975.

Greenwood, Peter W. *Disposition of Felony Arrests: The Effect of Prior Record and Estimates of Incapacitation Effects on Crime Rates.* Santa Monica, Calif.: Rand Corporation, June 1977. (R-2199-DOJ).

Hamparian, Donna Martin; Schuster, Richard; Dinitz, Simon and Conrad, John P. *The Violent Few*, Lexington, Mass.: Lexington Books, 1978.

Johnson, Perry M. "The Role of Penal Quarantine in Reducing Violent Crime," *Crime and Delinquency* 24(4):465-485, October, 1978.

Kassebaum, Gene; Ward, David and Wilner, Daniel. *Prison Treatment and Parole Survival.* New York: Wiley, 1971.

Lipton, Douglas; Martinson, Robert and Wilks, Judith. *The Effectiveness of Correctional Treatment.* New York: Praeger, 1975.

Marsh, Jeffrey and Singer, Max. *Soft Statistics and Hard Questions.* Hudson Institute, Discussion Paper HI-1712-DP, 1972.

Martinson, Robert. "What works?—questions and answers about prison reform," *The Public Interest* 35:22-54, Spring 1974.

Michael, Jerome and Adler, Mortimer J. *Crime, Law and Social Structure.* New York: Harcourt, Brace, 1933.

Monahan, John. "The Prediction of Violence," in *Violence and Criminal Justice*

(Duncan Chappell and John Monahan, eds.). Lexington, Mass.: Lexington Books, 1975.

Morris, Norval. *The Future of Imprisonment*. Chicago: The University of Chicago Press, 1974.

Murray, Charles A.; Thomson, Doug; Israel, Cindy B. *UDIS: Deinstitutionalizing the Chronic Juvenile Offender*, Washington, D.C.: American Institutes for Research, 1978.

Nagel, Jack H. "Crime and Incarceration: A Re-analysis," Fels Discussion Paper #112, Fels Center of Government, School of Public and Urban Policy, University of Pennsylvania, September, 1977.

Newman, Graeme. *The Punishment Response*. Philadelphia: Lippincott, 1978.

Palmer, Jan. "Economic Analysis of the Deterrence Effect of Punishment: A Review," *Journal of Research in Crime and Delinquency* 14(1):4-21, January, 1977.

Palmer, Jan, and Salimbene, John. "The Incapacitation of the Dangerous Offender: A Second Look," *Journal of Research in Crime and Delinquency* 15(1):130-134, January 1978.

Petersilia, Joan and Greenwood, Peter W. *Mandatory Prison Sentences: Their Projected Effects on Crime and Prison Populations*. Santa Monica, Calif.: Rand Corporation, August 1977.

Petersilia, Joan; Greenwood, Peter W. and Lavin, Marvin. *Criminal Careers of Habitual Offenders*. Santa Monica, Calif.: Rand, August, 1977.

Pfohl, Stephen. "The Psychiatric Assessment of Dangerousness," in *In Fear of Each Other* (John P. Conrad and Simon Dinitz, eds.), Lexington, Mass.: Lexington Books, 1977.

Radzinowicz, Leon. *Ideology and Crime*. New York: Columbia University Press, 1966.

Radzinowicz, Leon. *The Growth of Crime*. New York: Basic Books, 1977.

Rennie, Ysabel. *The Search for Criminal Man*. Lexington, Mass.: Lexington Books, 1978.

Shinnar, Reuel and Shinnar, Shlomo. "The Effects of the Criminal Justice System on the Control of Crime," *Law and Society Review* 9(4):581-611, 1975.

Silberman, Charles E. *Criminal Violence, Criminal Justice*, New York: Random House, 1978.

Sleffel, Linda. *The Law and the Dangerous Criminal*. Lexington, Mass.: Lexington Books, 1977.

Stephen, James Fitzjames. *History of the Criminal Law of England*. New York: Burt Franklin, 1883.

Sourcebook of Criminal Justice Statistics. 1974, 1975, 1976, 1977, 1978.

Uniform Crime Reports. 1970, 1971, 1972, 1973, 1974, 1975, 1976, 1977.

United States Census of Population and Housing: 1970-Columbus, Ohio.

van den Haag, Ernest. *Punishing Criminals: Concerning a Very Old and Painful Question*. New York: Basic Books, 1975.

Van Dine, Stephan W.; Conrad, John P. and Dinitz, Simon. "The Incapacitation of the Chronic Thug," *Journal of Criminal Law and Criminology*, in press.

Van Dine, Stephan W.; Dinitz, Simon and Conrad, John P. "The Incapacitation of the Dangerous Offender: A Statistical Experiment," *Journal of Research in Crime and Delinquency* 14(1):22-34, January 1977.

Van Dine, Stephan W.; Dinitz, Simon and Conrad, John P. "The Incapacitation of the Danger Offender: Response to Our Critics," *Journal of Research in Crime and Delinquency* 15(1):135-139, January 1978.

von Hirsch, Andrew. *Doing Justice*. New York: Hill and Wang, 1976.

von Hirsch, Andrew. "Prediction of Criminal Conduct and Preventive Confinement of Convicted Persons," *Buffalo Law Review* 21(3):717-758, Spring, 1972.

Walker, Nigel. "Review of Doing Justice by Andrew Von Hirsch," *British Journal of Criminology* 18(1):79-84, January 1978.

Wenk, Ernst; Robison, James and Smith, Gerald. "Can Violence be Predicted?" *Crime and Delinquency* 18(4):393-402, October 1972.

Wilson, James Q. "Changing Criminal Sentences," *Harpers* 255(5):16-20, November, 1977.

Wilson James Q. *Thinking About Crime*. New York: Basic Books, 1975.

Wilson, James Q. and Boland, Barbara. "Crime" in William Borham and Nathan Glazer (eds.), *The Urban Predicament*, Washington, D.C.: Urban Institute, 1976.

Wolfgang, Marvin E. "From Boy to Man—From Delinquency to Crime," Unpublished paper, presented at the National Symposium on the Serious Juvenile Offender, Minneapolis, Minn.: September 19-20, 1977.

Wolfgang, Marvin E. and Collins, James J., Jr., *Offender Careers and Restraint: Probabilities and Policy Implications*. Final Report to the National Institute of Juvenile Justice and Delinquency Prevention, 1977.

Wolfgang, Marvin E.; Figlio, Robert M. and Sellin, Thorsten. *Delinquency in a Birth Cohort*. Chicago: University of Chicago Press, 1972.

Index

Adult cohort, 5, 36, 37, 39, 41, 42, 47-48, 53, 56, 60, 64, 83, 88, 97-98; adult and juvenile cohort, 97-98; age, 37, 56; charges, 42; charges per defendant, 56; Columbus childhood, 82; convictions, 47-48; crimes cleared by, 36, 48; juvenile convictions, 83; juvenile records, 64; prior felony convictions, 37, 39, 41, 43, 56, 60; policy 4, adults with juvenile records, 83; race, 36, 56; sex, 36; socioeconomic status, 37; study population, 53, 88

age, 37, 39, 56, 90, 99, 114; adult cohort, 37; false-positives cohort, 99; juvenile cohort, 90; maturation, 114; and prior convictions, 39, 56

arrest assumption, 54

arrest level estimate, 62-63, 92-93; juvenile cohort, 92-93, 96; policy 4, adult cohort, 62-63

Beccaria, Cesare, 3

Bentham, Jeremy, 2, 3, 4, 9, 10, 14; on incapacitation, 3

Blumstein, Alfred, 13, 14, 31

"burn-out." See maturation

Career records, 36, 37; adult cohort, 36; defined, 36; felony convictions, 37

chronic offenders, 19, 20, 22, 32, 39, 41-42; and age, 39; defined, 19, 20

Clarke, Stevens, 29, 30, 33, 64

clearance, 12-13, 15, 36, 59, 60-61, 93-94; adult cohort, 36, 59, 60-61; Columbus police definition, 12, 15; FBI definition, 12, 15; juvenile cohort, 93-94; study definition, 12

Cohen, Jacqueline, 13, 14, 25, 26, 27, 30, 31, 33

Collins, James J., Jr., 10, 15, 30

Conrad, John P., xiv, 32, 59, 60, 61, 88

conviction level estimate, 63, 97; juvenile cohort, 97; policy 4, adult cohort, 63

convictions, prior felony, 36, 37, 39, 43, 56, 60, 64, 91, 100; adult cohort, 36, 37, 39, 43, 56, 60; career, defined, 36; false-positives cohort, 100; juvenile cohort, 91; no prior convictions. See first-time offender

convictions, instant offense, 47-48, 94, 101-102; adult cohort, 47-48; false-positives cohort, 101-102; juvenile cohort, 94

corrections, functions of, 1-4, 11, 17, 18, 113-114, 124; deterrence, 1, 18; incapacitation, 1-4; intimidation, 3, 18, 124; reformation, 3; rehabilitation, 1, 11, 17, 18, 124; retribution, 113-114

crime patterns, 42, 61-62, 81, 91, 103-104; adult cohort, 42; false-positives cohort, 103-104; juvenile cohort, 91; spacing, 61-62, 81

crime rates, 7, 22, 24, 26, 35, 119-120; estimated rate by crime, 119-120; individual average (λ), 7, 22, 24, 26; maximum rate by crime, 119; reported, 35

crimes cleared, 12-13, 47-48, 93-94, 117-122; by adult cohort, 47-48; definition, 12-13; by juvenile cohort, 93-94; quadrants I and II, 117-122

crimes uncleared, 12-13, 22, 114, 118-122, definition, 12-13; estimates about, 22; by false-positives, 114; quadrants III and IV, 118-122

"crime-switching." See crime patterns

criminal justice system, 43-49, 50, 53-54, 100, 111, 113; efficiency, 23, 25; processing, 43-49, 53-54, 100, 113; subjectivity, 50; summary observations, 111

About the Authors

Stephan Van Dine, is research coordinator, Adult Parole Authority, Ohio Department of Rehabilitation and Corrections.

He received the bachelor's from Wheaton College in Illinois and the master's degree in public administration from The Ohio State University. Before joining the Adult Parole Authority, Stephan Van Dine was a research associate at the Academy for Contemporary Problems. While at the Academy, he directed the four incapacitation projects reported in this volume. Mr. Van Dine has also been involved in other policy action research—on Ohio's reintegration centers, the work furlough program, and on the impact of a proposed flat-term sentence law on Ohio's prison population.

He has previously been a consultant or researcher for the Franklin County, Ohio Sheriff's Department, the Portland, Oregon Police Department and in 1978 for Northeastern University where he assisted in the revision and presentation of a curriculum in criminal justice evaluation.

Simon Dinitz, professor of sociology, Ohio State University and senior fellow, Center on Crime and Justice, The Academy for Contemporary Problems is codirector of the Dangerous Offender Project.

He received the bachelor's degree from Vanderbilt University and the master's and doctoral degrees from the University of Wisconsin.

Dr. Dinitz is a professor of sociology and has been a member of The Ohio State University faculty since 1951. He has previously held a joint appointment at The Ohio State University as a research associate in psychiatry and was a visiting professor to the Universities of Tel Aviv, Wisconsin and Southern California.

Dr. Dinitz is the author or coauthor of thirteen books and numerous articles and reports. He received the American Psychiatric Association's Hofheimer Prize in 1967 for *Schizophrenics in the Community: An Experiment in the Prevention of Hospitalization.* In addition, he received awards for outstanding teaching including the OSU Alumni Award for Distinguished Teaching. In 1974 he received the Sutherland Award of the American Society of Criminology for outstanding contributions to that field.

Dr. Dinitz has been a member or trustee of numerous government and civic groups, including the United Nations Social Defense Research Institute, the American Sociological Association Section on Criminology, the Ohio Governor's Task Force on Corrections, the Ohio Task Force on Mental Health and Retardation, and the International Advisory Board of the Institute of Criminology of the University of Tel Aviv. He is a former president of the American Society of Criminology and a former editor of its journal, *Criminology*.

John P. Conrad has been senior fellow, Center on Crime and Justice of the Academy for Contemporary Problems. In March, 1979 he assumed the position of Senior Program Officer at the American Justice Institute. He remains as codirector of the Academy's Dangerous Offender Project.

He received the bachelor's degree in political science from the University of California and the master's degree in social service administration from the University of Chicago. He has held teaching appointments at the University of California at Davis and the University of Pennsylvania, and adjunct professor of sociology at The Ohio State University. He also served as a visiting expert at the United Nations Asia and Far East Institute for the Prevention of Crime and the Treatment of Offenders in Tokyo, Japan.

Before coming to the academy, Mr. Conrad was chief of the Center for Crime Prevention and Rehabilitation of the Law Enforcement Assistance Administration and a consultant to the National Advisory Commission on Criminal Justice Standards and Goals. A career criminologist who spent 20 years in the administration of the California Department of Corrections, Mr. Conrad's experience also includes work with the United States Bureau of Prisons, an appointment as a Senior Fulbright Fellow in criminology at the London School of Economics, and associate director of the International Survey of Corrections. In addition, he was a consultant to the President's Commission on Law Enforcement and the Administration of Justice. Mr. Conrad has written numerous papers and *Crime and Its Correction,* and was chief editor of the *Journal of Research in Crime and Delinquency* from 1974 to 1976.